Latin Ladles

Latin Ladles

fabulous soups & stews from
the king of nuevo Latino cuisine

douglas rodriguez

introduction by
maricel presilla
photography by
dennis galante

ten speed press
berkeley, california

in Loving memory of
tim johnson, a friend and beLiever

✝

and aLso in memory of
feLipe rojas-Lombardi, a man ahead of his time

Copyright © 1997 by Douglas Rodriguez. All rights reserved. No part of this book may be reproduced in any form, except brief excerpts for the purpose of review, without written permission of the publisher.

Ten Speed Press
Box 7123
Berkeley, California 94707

Library of Congress Cataloging-in-Publication Data
Rodriguez, Douglas.
  Latin ladles : fabulous soups & stews from the king of nuevo latino cuisine / Douglas Rodriguez ; introduction by Maricel Presilla ; photography by Dennis Galante.
      p.   cm.
   Includes index.
   ISBN 0-89815-851-6
   1. Soups. 2. Stews. 3. Cookery, Latin American. I. Title
TX757.R723 1997
641.8'13'098—dc21   97-31653
                                CIP

Distributed in Canada by Publishers Group West, in Australia by Simon & Schuster Australia, in New Zealand by Tandem Press, in South Africa by Real Books, in Southeast Asia by Berkeley Books, and in the United Kingdom and Europe by Airlift Books.

Edited by Lorena Jones.
Cover and text design by Nancy Austin.
Photography © 1997 by Dennis Galante, New York City.
Food styling by Mariann Sauvion, New York City.
Art © 1997 by Diana Reiss, Berkeley, California.
Painting on back cover flap © 1997 by Tim McCarron, New York City (212-244-1835).

Printed in Hong Kong

First printing, 1997

1 2 3 4 5 6 7 8 9 10 — 02 01 00 99 98 97

contents

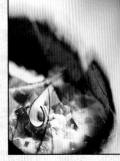

acknowledgments

Many thanks to all the people
who helped me create this book:

My beautiful wife, Trish, for everything

Our son, Leandro, and to Maricel Presilla
for constant inspiration

All my friends and employees at Patria,
who helped with recipe testing

Danielle Nally, for her wonderful typing

Aileen, for all the detailed research

Andrew Dicataldo, for testing and editing recipes

Keith Stupell, for the photography props

Dennis Galante, for the dynamic photography

And, at Ten Speed, thanks to Phil, Kirsty, Lorena, and
Nancy, without whose support and encouragement,
this book would not have been possible

CUBA
PUERTO RICO
DOMINICAN REPUBLIC
HAITI

GUATEMALA
HONDURAS
EL SALVADOR
NICARAGUA
PANAMA

COLOMBIA
VENEZUELA

ECUADOR

PERU

BRAZIL

BOLIVIA

CHILE

PARAGUAY

ARGENTINA

N

finding solidarity in the ladle and the pot

by maricel e. presilla

If Douglas Rodriguez and I were on a journey together through Latin America, we might seem unlikely traveling companions. Here and there, each of us would dart to a different side of the road, drawn toward new treasures. And yet somehow, as cooks, we would discover the same fabulous roots and pleasures of Latin cooking. At the end of the day, we would catch our breath and compare notes over the same steaming pot of soup.

In a soup pot something tremendous happens: The pot takes charge, taming what needs to be tamed, melting what needs to be melted. The pot is like a womb, forgiving and expanding to meet the new. It is the place where a slow simmer eases the transformation from the exotic to the familiar.

Restaurants that translate ethnic cuisines for the wider public, such as Douglas Rodriguez's Patria in New York City and Aguarela in Puerto Rico, are like great soup pots. They make the strange and alien more palatable. For many North Americans, visiting an ethnic neighborhood, with all its raw, pungent smells and unfamiliar languages, can be daunting. These places move to their own rhythms and passions, and it's hard to find somebody to translate or take you by the hand and steer you to the right lunch counter.

A handful of North American restaurateurs, such as Rick Bayless and Barbara Tropp, have popularized ethnic cuisines in this country, creating an artful balance between respectfulness and accessibility. Chef Felipe Rojas-Lombardi, to whom this book is partly dedicated, was a pioneer in bringing an Iberoamerican style of cooking to the United States in the early 1980s. His stylish Manhattan restaurant, The Ballroom, became the first showcase for Spanish tapas. The small dishes he created were not mere replicas of those served in Spanish tapas bars: They ranged from the traditional Spanish shrimp in garlic sauce to quinoa salad to morsels of Peruvian-style suckling pig. As Felipe explored his Peruvian roots while testing recipes for his last cookbook *The Art of South American Cooking*, more Latin dishes began to crop up on The Ballroom's menu. At the long bar counter, alongside the Galician-style octopus, one could find a huge black kettle bubbling with a different Latin soup every night—a luscious *puchero*, a creamy seafood *chupe*, and even a *caldo de patas*, a hearty Ecuadorean cow's hoof soup. Had Felipe not died at such an early age, his restaurant would have continued to evolve as part of this Latin American food revolution.

Chef Douglas Rodriguez belongs to this same company. With his bold and fanciful interpretations, Douglas has found ways to translate Latin cuisine for the passionate diner. He has created a homeland for his inventive palate, enticing Latinos and North Americans to visit. But Patria, with its Caribbean yellow walls and cobalt blue plates, is not a Latin theme park. It is a sophisticated restaurant that boldly presents new forms of Latin food without angst.

In a sense, Douglas is very much a part of North American culture, where tradition is a source of inspiration, yet is also turned on its head. In the irreverent soil of the United States, an imagination such as Douglas's is allowed to flourish in new and surprising forms. As a Latino born in the United States, Douglas has drawn on his Cuban background, but transformed it with a playful and freewheeling style. At the same time, he is distinctly part of a long lineage of Latin American criollo cooking, a hybrid cuisine that mingles old and new.

For Latin Americans, soup is as predictable as the sunrise. All over Latin America we begin our meals with soup, or soup becomes the meal itself. Historically, the all-embracing soup pot is where food traditions first mingled to give birth to a new *criollo* cuisine. The Spaniards were people of the hearth and came to the New World with their penchant for substantial soups, the medieval "putrid pot," *olla podrida,* so called because it was "filthy" rich with pork, chicken, sausages, white beans, and tubers like turnips and parsnips. They met other peoples—the Arawak or Taino, the Aztec, the Maya, the Aymara, the Inca, the African—

who were also soup, stew, and porridge makers. In the New World pot, seemingly incompatible ingredients came together: Hot peppers—chiles and *ajíes*—gave pungency to meats, noodles, and rice from the Old World; *achiote* won out over saffron in seducing and gilding the chicken; pork and lard gave a satiny texture to coarse cornmeal porridges; tubers like yuca, malanga, and potatoes joined and even came to replace Old World vegetables in the "putrid pot."

The Spanish and Portugese arrived in the New World craving the foods they remembered. But like all immigrants, they were marked by the moment of transition, when they surrendered to the realities of weather and geography and reached for substitutions. Thus, the sixteenth-century Castillians and Extremadurans who once ate from a cauldron bubbling with chickpeas, white beans, parsnips, turnips and cabbage, found themselves adding yuca or calabaza and coloring with achiote. The nineteenth-century Portuguese plantation owner was hypnotically drawn to the cavernous kitchen where his African-born cook stirred a sultry *feijoada.* At the turn of the century, the white bean–loving Catalan reached out for the black beans, red beans, and cranberry beans. And the Galician immigrant of the 1920s shook his head in disapproval when his Cuban wife turned the thin *caldo gallego* of his memory into a soup as thick as a stew, but then he asked for seconds. Soon the substitutions, the foods of the land, and the brand new creations became comforting. This is the moment of creolization or *aplatanamiento,* when the alien, like the African plantain, becomes native, a familiar sight and flavor in the all-inclusive pot of the New World.

Likewise, the Andean farmers who made *mote* (hominy) soups with no fat—found themselves following the Spaniards' techniques, such as flavoring with pork and *sofrito*. The West Africans, who made yam and plantain porridges called *fufu*, and the Guinea-coast Africans, who cooked rice and beans, now found themselves working the plantations and eating austere rations of salt cod and beef jerky. Soon they were allowed to supplement their diets with New World vegetables and tubers like yuca, sweet potatoes, pumpkins, corn and the familiar African yam, plantains, and okra which they grew in their small *conucos*, or gardens. To this, they added the velvety, smooth milk of coconuts, which eventually enriched all the African-inspired cuisines of tropical American.

From the Rio Grande to the tip of South America, one finds *pucheros, locros, sancochos, ajiacos, chupes, biches,* and *carbonadas*—bountiful soups and stews that bring together several meats and starches, and even boast surprising combinations. Take the *carbonada criolla*, a hefty stew from the northwestern provinces of Argentina that is really a one-pot meal with chunks of corn, ripe peaches, sweet potatoes, and beef served from a scooped-out pumpkin. This is a food that conjures up harvest and Mother Earth, anchoring you to the ground—you can climb a mountain after eating such a nourishing stew.

To a stranger, these one-pot meals, with their layers of starch upon starch, protein upon protein, might seem like a crowded bus. But Latin Americans know how each element works in achieving a culinary synthesis: In the *ajiaco bogotano*, Colombians use one type of potato because it will keep its shape, another because it will melt into the soup, adding body to the broth, and yet another for color and flavor. To make a *sancocho*, Hispanic Caribbean cooks add yuca because it imparts a subtle sweetness, *ocumo chino* (taro) because it melts into a creamy porridge-like consistency.

Hearty soups are a constant in Latin America. In the tropics, everyone needs a reason to stop and rest; otherwise you will melt under the scorching sun. People eat these lush soups at lunch to sweat and slow down, afterward taking refuge in a dark bedroom with shutters drawn, a hammock, or a shady verandah. In the windswept cold highlands of the Andes, thick soups made with freeze-dried potatoes and bits of lamb keep the potato farmer going, nourishing him so he can work until the sun sets behind the rugged peaks. Throughout Latin America, where fuel and kitchenware are often limited, the soup pot allows you to cook with an economy of means. With a pot, a spoon and a bowl, even the poorest can enjoy a rich meal.

All over Latin America, people say, "Come over this Sunday, I'm making a *puchero*, a *sancocho*, an *ajiaco*"—big soups that become magnets for family and friends, their unabashed enjoyment a ritual that crosses classes. These soups are not cowardly watery broths. In Latin America the distinction between soups, stews, and porridges is often blurry. Latins like their tubers, vegetables, and meats to melt together into a soup that is thick enough to cut with a knife. Nor is there anything delicate about the way these soups are eaten. Everyone gathers around the table, hunched over huge soup bowls heaped with steaming vegetables, meats, and tubers, getting up only to ladle more from the pot or to top their bowls with some rice.

In the Ecuadorean highlands, on any day in the market, one can see rows of people sitting at long tables, bent over their plates of piping soup, hot sauce on the side. They hold the bowls so close, and eat with such concentrated intensity, you can't even see their faces. Spirals of steam seem to be coming out of their ears. Everywhere in the Hispanic Caribbean, from the Greater Antilles to Paria in Venezuela, muscular, shirtless men and voluptuous women in shorts and tank tops stand outside in their backyards or along the roadside, cooking *sancochos* in huge cauldrons. While the chicken and meat slowly simmers, mounds of cut-up golden pumpkin and bone-white yuca, large as elephant tusks, overflow metal wash basins, waiting to be added to the pot. When the soup is ready, it is unceremoniously ladled into anything that can hold liquid—worn-out enameled bowls, or even hollowed-out, dried gourds.

And then there are the Latin soups that magically bear offspring. Regardless of their humble beginnings in the kitchens of slaves and peasants, these baroque soups often become the basis of holiday meals and lavish entertainment. Take the Peruvian *puchero* or the *feijoada*, Brazil's national dish, an elaborate black bean soup enriched with layer upon layer of smoked and salted beef and pork—tongue, pork's feet, tail, sausages, and ears. Like the Portuguese *cozido*, each ingredient is served separately—the bean soup in a tureen, the meats, beautifully arranged on a large platter around the thinly sliced beef

tongue. At the end, everything comes back together on a single, gargantuan plate.

When trying to explain the origins of big soups such as the *feijoada*, you often hear that slaves used all parts of the animal that the masters had discarded. In truth, in Latin America, everyone—from slaves to masters to Indians—relished and enjoyed parts of the animal that might make some squeamish in North America. The proof is that even today, many of Latin America's favorite soups and stews still brim with tripe, pigs' feet, ears, bones, and cows' hooves.

When it comes to fish, those in the know go for the most flavorful part—the head. In coastal communities all over Latin America, fishermen reserve fish heads to make strong soups. Everywhere, these mighty, concentrated brews are jokingly called "*levanta muertos*," soups that revive the dead. In Chile, a country with strong fishing traditions, people gather strength after a night of drinking and partying by sipping fish soup for breakfast. Fishermen with glossy, black hair sit down near the port or the marketplace to enjoy soup dishes with lavish combinations of shellfish and fish—*picorocos, machas*, clams, *corvina*. Any restaurant has these nourishing power soups, with their riotous concatenations of seafood. Since seafood is considered to have aphrodisiac powers, Chileans dub these potent concoctions "mating soups."

It is telling that an eclectic cook like Felipe Rojas-Lombardi, who had an enormous curiosity about many ethnic cuisines, never lost his fascination for the soup pot. The pot became the active culture for his own inventiveness, where he mingled ingredients and techniques from the cuisines he admired. At The Ballroom, Felipe served samplings of his deeply flavored, gem-like soups in small espresso cups—a clever way to enjoy a variety of soups as tapas. At the core of his soups, though, was his criollo identity, as demonstrated in his deft use of the sofrito, the gilding of achiote, the balance between sweet and sour flavorings, and the tart kiss of lime juice, the finishing touch of many Latin American soups.

Like Felipe Rojas-Lombardi, Douglas Rodriguez's cooking is also driven by the criollo impulse; he, too, represents the moment when the immigrant adopts substitutions, changing old habits to embrace new ideas and tastes. Many of the soups in this book are traditional, pure criollo. Others show the imprint of the enlarging North American market basket, bearing the touch of our adoptive *patria chica,* bountiful Manhattan, a new Tenochtitlán, with its dizzying range of ingredients and aesthetic possiblities.

Though one might suspect that Douglas's loyalties lie with his father's red-bean soup, he's too curious to ladle from one pot. He does not choose ingredients, colors, and textures according to tradition and geography. Instead he borrows freely across borders, combining foods never before seen together. Once, when visiting a market in Santo Domingo in the Dominican Republic, Douglas spotted a display of well-known aphrodisiacs. He brought back a hundred of these bottles and used the liquid in his *ceviches*—"just a few drops," he liked to say, with a mischievous twinkle in his eyes. It's this canny instinct to recognize the potential in unusual ingredients that is the strength of Douglas's adventurous talent.

At home, Douglas serves hearty soups unadorned. But when he transports these homey soups to his restaurants, they give you a jolt of surprise. They are like surreal flying saucers skidding off the Latin American map, flashing with alien and familiar flavors. Highly stylized, his creations zoom from the kitchen to the dining table, their vaporous tails of history trailing. Douglas's soups aren't ephemeral or fleeting, though. These soups may fly, but like all good Latin soups, they also land safely, embracing you with their earthy warmth.

To make his soups and stews, Douglas uses many traditional ingredients such as yuca, malanga, boniato, and calabaza, which we all grew up with in the Hispanic Caribbean, and techniques such as the *sofrito.* But his flavor palate is Pan-American. If he wants a smoky flavor, he will use Mexican chipotle in an Argentinean *carbonada,* taking it to a place where the influence of Mexico no longer exists. He stretches the possibilities, turning a *serenata,* a hearty Puerto Rican cod salad, into a satisfying ladle dish.

Douglas also knows how to make artful presentations that appeal to American food aesthetics. In Latin America pea soups are intensely flavored yet not necessarily bright in color, but Douglas's pea soup is an almost comic-book green, a pop-art splash of color. One of my favorite soups in this book is a Dominican-inspired bone-marrow soup. For Latins, nothing is more familiar than huge pieces of bone giving flavor to a soup, but the bones seldom make it to the table. In Douglas's version, the bone thrusts from the bowl like a brazen sculpture.

Some traditional Latin soups, such as

chicken-noodle soup, are soothing, meant to warm you up or pave the way for more substantial fare. Douglas, though, adds an extra-sharp kick to his soups that appeals to the American palate. It's as if he has taken someone who usually dons work clothes and stays at home, dressed her up with panache and flair, and brought her outside for a stroll. Douglas has also explored the range of one-pot meals. Some are plain and nourishing stews and porridges, like the Cuban *tamal en cazuela,* as if served piping hot off his mother's Oriente stove. Others are injected with a high-voltage current.

Like a restaurant, a cookbook is a passport and map to a once inscrutable ethnic neighborhood. Once upon a time, Latin cookbooks were full of compromises because authentic ingredients were hard to come by. Usually cooks ended up with dishes that made use of more familiar Mediterranean components, safe spices, and tomato sauces. But other cuisines have since made their mark on America, introducing many crossover tropical foods that are also found in Latin cooking. One can go to gourmet stores and find sweet potatoes, plantains, papaya, and passion fruit. But the real treasures are found in Latin neighborhoods. Nowadays Latin markets are chock-full of a breathtaking array of ingredients from all over the Americas: tropical tubers grown in Florida, Peruvian freeze-dried potatoes, a whole range of Mexican dried peppers, as well as lesser-known Andean peppers such as *ají mirasol,* a pepper so versatile it's tempting to use it in everything.

People from Latin America hold fast to their culinary heritages. Latinos belong to a house, a town, a region, taking pride in the range of flavors of the small countries they have created in their kitchens. Certainly, it's important to preserve the old ways, the time-tested recipes handed down from generation to generation. But now there are two Latin Americas: one that is geography bound and steeped in tradition, the other, a fast-changing construct created by immigration. Here in the United States, Latin Americans have been thrust together, which offers the opportunity for accelerated stretching and mingling of traditions. We live in areas where Cuban *boniatos* and guava paste are sold side-by-side with Andean corn and quinoa. It's hard not to reach out our hands and borrow, impossible to resist the siren's call to experiment. Go into the kitchens of many New York restaurants, and often you'll find that staff members come from all over Latin America. Not surprisingly, some of Douglas's recipes are drawn from his own employees, who are constantly learning from each other.

Soups and stews are a perfect way to ease into a new cuisine. Since the pot is so forgiving, soup making is good for novices and experienced cooks alike. But making a Latin soup or stew isn't just about adding and mixing the new and the familiar. It's also an irresistible invitation to the Latin American experience. Latin Americans are people of the pot. For centuries, entire families and friends have been gathering around their worn-out iron cauldrons brimming with cornmeal porridge or clay pots filled with broth and potatoes, finding solidarity in the ladle and the pot. To dip your ladle into a pot and serve up your *own* Latin American soup or stew is to participate in this age-old ritual of communion.

LaðLe Notes

As you read my recipes, please keep a few things in mind:

* Many of them call for a squeeze of lime juice over the soup just before eating. This is a common practice throughout Latin America and essential to the full enjoyment of the recipes.

* I've purposely given descriptive English names, not literal translations of the Spanish titles, for each of the soups. I think it's more important that you know exactly what you're cooking than that you brush up on your Spanish. And for the Spanish, I've chosen to use the vernacular names that I've heard the soups and stews called in the kitchens of New York, Miami, the Caribbean, and Central and South America, rather than the formal titles you might learn in a cooking school. In some cases, I've broken ranks completely and given them my own names.

* You may come across many ingredients that are new to your kitchen. For more about them and where to buy them, see pages 122–124.

* I consider a single serving to be approximately $1^1/_2$ cups of soup or stew. For a light soup, that's enough to be a substantial starter; with heartier soups and stews, that's enough for a main course or, in many cases, a full meal.

These recipes come from my heart. They have evolved out of years of traveling, cooking, eating, and experimenting, as well as from my reverence for Latin America's ancient and ever-changing cuisines. You will find that these dishes are easy to make and require only basic ingredients, yet have an entirely different taste than anything you've had before—that's the Latin flavor coming through. I have enjoyed most of these soups and stews (some many times) with my friends and family at home as well as at both restaurants. I know these recipes have a way of filling a kitchen with good smells, lively conversation, and booming laughter. I am proud and pleased to share them, and hope they bring the same joys to your kitchen.

sancocho

sopa de rabo

pepián de pavo

jocón

sopa de médula

guiso de malanga
y carne de vaca

sopa de albóndigas

sopa de carne de
cerdo y papa

ajiaco bogotano

meat- and poultry-based soups

SANCOCHO
[simple chicken and
vegetable stew]

Sancocho is the national dish of Santo Domingo. Variations of it are also common throughout Venezuela and other Latin American countries; the recipes vary a lot from region to region. This one was given to me verbally while I was researching and developing recipes for this book, and I've since tested and adjusted it quite a few times. *Sancochar* means "to stew" or "boil" in Spanish, and this one-pot meal is the Latin American version of New England's boiled dinners. It uses a fair amount of ingredients, but it's worth the extra effort—the finished dish is very hearty and rich.

SERVES 4

1 gallon chicken stock, including whole cooked chicken (page 116)

Sofrito (page 115)

2 potatoes, peeled and cut into large dice

1 pound yuca, peeled and diced

$^{1}/_{2}$ pound malanga, peeled and diced

2 ears corn, cut crosswise into $^{1}/_{2}$-inch-wide slices

2 green plantains, peeled and diced

1 ripe plantain, peeled and diced

1 lime, quartered

1. Prepare a grill.

2. In a large stockpot over medium heat, combine the stock and sofrito. Remove the fat from the chicken, then carefully pull the meat off the bones in large strands. Place the strands of chicken on the hot grill and cook until golden brown.

3. Add the potatoes, yuca, malanga, corn, plantains, and chicken strips to the stockpot. Cook and stir about 40 minutes.

4. Ladle the stew into bowls and serve with the lime wedges on the side. Squeeze lime juice over the stew before eating.

sopa de rabo
[oxtail soup]

If you've never had oxtail before, this soup is a great introduction to it. It's very important to cook the oxtail for at least 2½ to 3 hours, until the meat is falling off the bone, and to skim all the fat off the top of the soup (oxtail has a lot of fat on it). If you can't find dandelion greens, you may substitute collard greens, Swiss chard, or even beet greens. I've added balsamic vinegar to what was basically a classic recipe from Uruguay, because I think the soup needs the little zing the vinegar gives. You might serve it with roasted potatoes on the side.

SERVES 4 TO 6

3 pounds oxtail, cut into 2-inch-thick rounds

½ cup flour, seasoned with a pinch of salt and pepper

3 tablespoons achiote oil

1 white onion, diced

6 cloves garlic, chopped

4 jalapeño chiles, stemmed and diced (including seeds)

2 ounces fresh ginger, peeled and minced

1 gallon beef stock (page 115)

1 teaspoon chipotle chile powder

1 tablespoon dried oregano

6 plum tomatoes, peeled, seeded, and diced (page 121)

8 ounces dandelion greens, julienned

Salt and freshly ground black pepper

4 tablespoons balsamic vinegar

1. In a mixing bowl, toss the oxtail rounds with the seasoned flour until evenly coated.

2. Heat the achiote oil in a large stockpot over high heat. Add the oxtail pieces and brown well on all sides, about 12 minutes. Add the onion, garlic, jalapeños, and ginger. Cook for 5 minutes, then add the stock and bring to a boil.

3. When boiling, decrease the heat to low, cover, and simmer for about 2½ hours.

4. Uncover and skim off any fat or impurities that may have risen to the surface of the soup. Add the chile powder and oregano. Simmer uncovered for about 20 minutes. Stir in the tomatoes and greens, season to taste with salt and pepper, and simmer for about 10 minutes.

5. Ladle the soup into bowls, drizzle each with some of the balsamic vinegar, and serve.

pepián de pavo
[turkey in chile sauce]

This dish, and its many variations, is popular throughout Central America. It can be made with a green or red sauce. This version is a red style, with red chiles and tomatoes. If you want to make it green, just omit the red chiles. Although its name is derived from the Spanish word *pepa*, meaning "seed," its roots are actually Maya. The soup is traditionally made with turkey, but you can use duck, chicken, Cornish hens, or any game bird of your choice.

SERVES 4 TO 6

1 gallon chicken stock (page 116)
1 two-pound boneless turkey breast
1 teaspoon salt
1 white onion, diced
4 cloves garlic
3 bay leaves
3 jalapeño chiles, stemmed
1 tablespoon achiote oil (page 115)
8 ripe plum tomatoes, diced
5 ounces tomatillos, husked, rinsed in warm water, and chopped
3 pasilla chiles, stemmed and seeded
3 ancho chiles, stemmed and seeded
1/4 cup pumpkin seeds
1 tablespoon coriander seeds
1 teaspoon cumin seeds
1 tablespoon crushed red pepper flakes
1 tablespoon whole allspice
1 cinnamon stick, chopped

1. Combine stock, turkey breast, salt, onion, garlic, bay leaves, and jalapeños in a large stockpot over high heat. Bring the mixture to a boil, then decrease the heat, cover, and simmer about 50 minutes.

2. Remove the turkey breast from the stockpot and set aside to cool. Add the oil, tomatoes, tomatillos, and chiles to the stockpot.

3. When the turkey is cool, shred it, using one fork to anchor the meat and the other to tear it off the breast into small strips.

4. In a dry skillet over medium heat, toast the pumpkin seeds and spices until they begin to darken around the edges and release their aromas. Turn the seeds and spices out onto a plate and let cool. When cool, grind into a fine powder in a spice grinder. Add the powder to the stockpot.

5. Simmer the soup for 15 minutes. Purée with a handheld blender until smooth. Add the turkey strips and simmer 5 more minutes.

6. Ladle into bowls and serve.

jocón
[duck in green stew]

This dish is interesting because the acidity of the tomatillos and the sauce itself counterbalances the richness of the duck. It's especially good served with white rice (see page 114) or fresh sweet corn.

SERVES 4

3 tablespoons shelled pumpkin seeds

1 tablespoon shelled sunflower seeds

1 tablespoon coriander seeds

1 whole duck, split, backbone removed, and quartered

Salt and freshly ground black pepper

1 tablespoon olive oil

1 white onion, diced

3 cloves garlic, chopped

1 quart chicken stock (page 116) or water

5 dried cobán chiles, or 3 chipotle chile peppers

6 ounces tomatillos, husked and rinsed in warm water

3/4 cup tightly packed cilantro leaves

2 bunches green onions, white and green parts thinly sliced

1. Preheat the oven to 400°.

2. In a dry skillet over low heat, toast the pumpkin, sunflower, and coriander seeds until they are lightly browned and begin to crackle loudly. Turn out onto a plate and let cool. When cool, grind finely in a spice grinder.

3. Place a baking dish in the oven and heat for 25 minutes. Meanwhile, season the duck generously with salt and pepper. Heat the olive oil in a large skillet over medium heat. Place the duck, skin side down, in the pan. Brown well on one side, then turn. Set the dusk breasts aside. Place the legs in the heated baking dish and return to the oven for 20 minutes, then let cool in the fat that has collected in the dish.

4. Heat 3 tablespoons of the duck fat in a large stockpot over medium heat. Add the onion and garlic and saute until the onion is translucent, stirring often, about 6 minutes. Add the toasted seeds, stock, and coban peppers. Bring to a boil and let boil 5 minutes. Decrease the heat and simmer for 30 minutes. Remove from the heat.

5. Place 1 cup of the stock in a blender and add the tomatillos, cilantro, and green onions. Purée until smooth. Pour the puréed mixture into the stockpot. Add the duck and simmer 10 minutes. Taste and adjust seasonings, if necessary.

6. Ladle the soup into bowls and serve.

sopa de médula
[bone marrow soup]

Bone marrow soup is a classic enjoyed in many countries, not just in Latin America. It's very rich yet light at the same time, and the fine noodles make it elegant. One of the ways to make it even more elegant is to clean the bones for the garnish very well, scraping them with a knife until they are perfectly clean.

SERVES 4

 5 quarts veal stock (page 120)

 3 bay leaves, crushed

 2 teaspoons dried oregano

 $^1/_2$ teaspoon black peppercorns

 6 three-inch veal marrow bones

 2 small carrots, peeled and cut crosswise into thin slices

 $^1/_2$ cup chopped shallots

 1 red onion, diced

 8 cloves garlic, crushed

 5 ounces dried angel hair pasta

 1 malanga, diced

 $^1/_2$ cup freshly squeezed sour (Seville) orange juice

 1 cup dry sherry

 1 tablespoon chopped flat-leaf parsley

 2 tablespoons chopped fresh cilantro leaves

1. In a stockpot over high heat, bring the stock to a boil. Add the bay leaves, oregano, peppercorns, and marrow bones. Decrease heat to low and cook uncovered until bones look translucent, 35 to 40 minutes.

2. Remove the bones from the stockpot and set aside. Add the carrots, shallots, onion, and garlic and cook 15 minutes.

3. Pour the liquid through a fine-mesh strainer and return to the stockpot, discarding the vegetables and spices.

4. Add the pasta, malanga, orange juice, sherry, and reserved bones to the stockpot. Cook until heated through, 3 to 4 minutes. Stir in the parsley and cilantro.

5. Ladle into bowls and serve.

guiso de malanga y carne de vaca
[malanga and beef stew]

Malanga, one of my favorite tubers, has an earthy, almost grassy flavor and is a member of the taro root family. There are several kinds of malangas. My favorite is called *malanga coco,* which looks like a yellow crookneck squash with a hairy coconut shell and has a mushroomy flavor. This hearty stew is perfect for cold winter days, along with a glass of robust red wine.

SERVES 4

1 pound malanga, peeled and diced

1 quart water

2 cups milk

3 tablespoons olive oil

1 pound ground beef

1 white onion, diced

4 plum tomatoes, diced

4 cloves garlic, diced

1 red bell pepper, diced

2 jalapeño chiles, stemmed and diced (including seeds)

1 teaspoon dried oregano

1. In a medium stockpot, combine the malanga, water, and milk. Bring the mixture to a boil, decrease the heat, cover, and simmer 20 minutes. Uncover and purée with a handheld blender.

2. Heat the oil in a large sauté pan over high heat. Add the ground beef and break up with a spoon, stirring until well browned, about 8 minutes. Add the onion, tomatoes, garlic, bell pepper, jalapeños, and oregano. Cook about 10 minutes, stirring less frequently. Add to malanga purée, stir well and let simmer 10 minutes.

3. Ladle the soup into bowls and serve.

sopa de albóndigas
[meatball soup]

Albóndigas literally means "meatballs," and they're what give this peasant-style soup its character. This is a particularly interesting recipe because of the mustard in the meatballs. It's the mustard that gives the soup that pungent, peppery aroma as it cooks.

SERVES 4

1 pound ground beef

2 cloves garlic, minced

1/2 small white onion, finely diced

1 teaspoon Colman's dry mustard

2 tablespoons chopped fresh flat-leaf parsley

1 tablespoon dried oregano

1 tablespoon tomato paste

2 tablespoons milk

2 tablespoons bread crumbs

1 teaspoon salt

1 teaspoon ground white pepper

1 gallon beef stock (page 115)

2 carrots, peeled and sliced

1 bunch green onions, white and green parts thinly sliced

1/2 cup fresh or frozen peas

4 jalapeño chiles, stemmed and thinly sliced crosswise (including seeds)

1. In a large mixing bowl, combine the ground beef, garlic, onion, dry mustard, parsley, oregano, tomato paste, milk, bread crumbs, salt, and white pepper. Shape into small meatballs (about 20), and set aside.

2. In a large stockpot over medium-high heat, bring the stock and carrots to a boil. Decrease the heat to low and simmer for 10 minutes.

3. Add the meatballs to the simmering stock one at a time and let cook 15 minutes. Add the green onions, peas, and jalapeños, and simmer 10 more minutes.

4. Ladle into bowls and serve.

sopa de carne de cerdo y papa
[pork and potato soup]

This is a one-pot meal from Venezuela. Make sure the pork is cooked at a very high heat, so that the outside of the meat is well caramelized and completely browned. Precooking the achiote oil gives the meat a slightly nutty flavor and turns the meat reddish. It also intensifies any sweetness in the meat and other ingredients. Try it out.

SERVES 4 TO 6

2 tablespoons achiote oil

3 pounds lean pork loin, trimmed and cut into $^1/_2$-inch chunks

1 white onion, diced

6 cloves garlic, chopped

4 large potatoes, peeled and cut into $^1/_2$-inch chunks

3 cups beef stock (page 115)

1 teaspoon dried oregano

1 tablespoon capers

4 plum tomatoes

Salt and freshly ground black pepper

1. Heat the achiote oil in a large, high-sided skillet over high heat. Add the pork and brown for about 6 minutes while continuously stirring. Add the onion and garlic and cook 3 more minutes. Add the potatoes and stock and cover. Bring the mixture to a boil. Decrease the heat to low, cover, and simmer for about 15 minutes.

2. Uncover the stockpot and add the oregano, capers, and tomatoes. Season to taste with salt and pepper. Stir and cook for 5 more minutes.

3. Ladle the soup into bowls and serve.

ajiaco bogotano
[creamy potato and chicken soup]

I'm told that this is the most popular dish in Bogotá, the capital of Colombia. It gets much of its distinctive flavor from *guasca,* which is an herb typically used in Colombia. Here in New York, I buy it in the barrio. It's not like any other herb I've ever had. It comes in powder form and has an artichokelike flavor. This recipe was given to me by an employee's mother, who actually came to the restaurant and cooked it for me. I get so excited when I talk about this soup that I never know where to start. It has a rich, earthy sweetness, and when you take a bite along with some sour cream and capers, you get a little punch. It's an absolutely wonderful soup and a meal on its own.

SERVES 4 TO 6

1 gallon chicken stock (page 116)

4 large skinless, boneless chicken breast halves with fat

2 1/2 pounds yellow fingerling potatoes, well scrubbed

2 pounds Yukon gold potatoes, well scrubbed and cut into 1/2-inch chunks

1 pound white turnips, peeled and diced

3 carrots, peeled and sliced

3 ears sweet corn, cut crosswise into 1-inch-wide pinwheels

1 cup heavy cream

2 tablespoons guasca

1 tablespoon chopped cilantro leaves

1 bunch green onions, white and green parts thinly sliced

1 cup fresh or frozen peas

1/2 cup sour cream

3 tablespoons capers

1. In a large stockpot over high heat, bring the stock, chicken, potatoes, turnips, and carrots to a boil. Let boil for 5 minutes, decrease the heat to low, add the corn, cover, and simmer for 25 minutes.

2. Stir in the cream. Remove the chicken breasts and set aside to cool.

3. While the chicken cools, continue to stir the soup as it cooks. Using two forks, shred the chicken. When the potatoes begin to fall apart, add the guasca, cilantro, green onions, and chicken. Cover, turn off the heat, and let rest for 10 minutes.

4. Add the peas and cook for 5 minutes.

5. Ladle the soup into bowls. Place a dollop of sour cream in the center of each bowl, sprinkle with capers, and serve.

sopa de manguera
[tripe soup]

Manguera means "hose," and this soup gets its name from the hoselike tripe in it. Tripe has a naturally rubbery texture, but Ecuadoreans purposely undercook it for this soup so it's extra rubbery. The first time I had the soup was at La Canoa, a restaurant in Guayaquil, Ecuador. It's the restaurant's daily lunch soup, and they make it in this big kettle set over bricks and twigs right there in the dining room. When I had the soup, I knew it was made with tripe, but I didn't know what made it black. After my wife and I finished the entire four-cup bowl of soup, which was delicious and had a nice spice, a rich flavor, and amazing aroma, we discovered it got its color, and probably much of its flavor, from pig's blood. We couldn't believe we liked it so much. If we'd known there was blood in it, we probably wouldn't have eaten it. Don't let yourself make that mistake. You can buy fresh or frozen pork blood from some Latin American and Asian butchers. There is no substitute.

SERVES 6 TO 8

1 pound honeycomb tripe

1 cup plus 2 tablespoons distilled white vinegar

5 bay leaves

1 tablespoon crushed red pepper flakes

1 tablespoon dried thyme

1 tablespoon dried oregano

8 cloves garlic

1 gallon water

$^1/_2$ cup achiote oil

1 red onion, cut into small dice

6 cloves garlic, diced

3 jalapeño chiles, stemmed and diced (including seeds)

1 small red bell pepper, diced

3 stalks celery, diced (about $^1/_2$ cup)

1 gallon chicken stock (page 116)

1 cup dry red wine

1 cup long-grain white rice

2 carrots, peeled and diced (about 1 cup)

1 teaspoon ground cumin

1 teaspoon dried oregano

4 plum tomatoes, diced

4 cups pork blood

1 pound chorizo, sliced $^1/_2$ inch thick

$^1/_4$ cup cilantro leaves

1. Thoroughly rinse the tripe under cold, running water. Fill a large bowl with ice water and add 2 tablespoons of the vinegar. Place the tripe in the bowl and let soak for 30 minutes. Remove from the water, pat dry, and cut into 1-inch cubes.

2. In a large stockpot, combine the tripe, bay leaves, pepper flakes, thyme, oregano, whole garlic cloves, water, and the remaining 1 cup of vinegar. Bring to a boil over high heat and cook at a full boil for 1 hour. Remove from the heat and let cool. Drain the tripe, rinse in cold water, and reserve.

3. Heat the achiote oil in a large stockpot over high heat. Add the onion, diced garlic, jalapeños, bell pepper, and celery and cook about 5 minutes. Add the chicken stock and wine. Bring to a boil. Add the rice and cook 15 minutes. Decrease the heat and simmer for 1 hour.

4. Add the carrots, reserved tripe, cumin, oregano, and tomatoes and cook for 10 minutes. Whisk in the blood. Stir in the chorizo.

5. Coarsely chop the cilantro. Ladle the soup into bowls. Garnish each bowl with a sprinkle of cilantro and serve.

ximxim
[brazilian chicken stew]

Pronounced "chimchim," this is a peas-
ant soup from northeastern Brazil. It
starts out as a basic chicken soup, but the
addition of peanuts and dried shrimp,
which are characteristic of Brazilian
cooking, thicken it into a stew. I like to
garnish it with freshly shredded coconut
and a squeeze of juice. For more about
dried shrimp, see page 123.

SERVES 6 TO 8

3 tablespoons dendê oil

2 pounds boneless chicken breasts,
   with skin, quartered

1 white onion, diced

1 red bell pepper, diced

8 to 10 cachucha peppers, stemmed,
   seeded, and chopped

4 jalapeño chiles, stemmed and diced
   (including seeds)

6 plum tomatoes, peeled and seeded
   (page 121)

6 cloves garlic

4 cups chicken stock (page 116)

1/2 cup roasted unsalted peanuts,
   coarsely ground

1/2 cup dried shrimp

1 12-ounce can coconut milk

1 to 1 1/2 pounds medium shrimp,
   peeled and deveined

8 sprigs cilantro

5 green onions, white and green parts
   sliced

Salt and freshly ground black pepper

1. Heat the dendê oil in a large stockpot
   over high heat. Place the chicken, skin
   side down, in the pot and brown well on
   both sides. Add the white onion, bell
   pepper, chiles, tomatoes, and garlic. Stir
   and cook about 10 minutes. Add stock
   and stir again. Add the peanuts and dried
   shrimp, stirring well. Cook another 10
   minutes. Add the coconut milk and cook
   another 10 minutes.

2. Ten minutes before serving, stir in the
   fresh shrimp. Julienne the cilantro leaves.
   Add the cilantro and green onions to
   the soup. Season to taste with salt and
   pepper.

3. Ladle the soup into bowls and serve.

puchero moderno
[modern everyday chicken stew]

Puchero is traditionally made with whole cabbage, carrots, and onions, but I make it with Brussels sprouts, baby carrots, and pearl onions because they are sweeter, more tender, and look more elegant than the full-sized vegetables. To eat this dish, alternate spoonfuls of broth and forkfuls of chicken and vegetables dipped in the mustard. Eating puchero is a ritual in itself—perfect for Sunday suppers.

SERVES 4

6 quarts water

1 whole chicken (about 3 pounds), rinsed well and patted dry

3 bay leaves

3 sprigs thyme

1 tablespoon black peppercorns

2 tablespoons kosher salt

2 ancho chiles, stemmed and seeded

Zest of 1 lemon

10 ounces white pearl onions

1 pound Brussels sprouts, trimmed and washed

9 ounces baby carrots, peeled

6 small red potatoes, scrubbed

5 leeks, white parts only, split and washed

3 chorizo sausages (about 1 pound)

2 tablespoons chopped flat-leaf parsley

Whole-grain mustard

1. In a large stockpot over high heat, bring the water, chicken, bay leaves, thyme, peppercorns, salt, and chiles to a boil. When boiling, decrease the heat to low, cover, and simmer for about $1^1/_2$ hours, periodically skimming off any fat and impurities that rise to the surface. Remove the chicken from the pot and transfer to a platter. Add the zest to the broth.

2. Bring a saucepan of water to a boil and prepare a small ice-water bath. Trim off the root end of the onions. Blanch the onions in the boiling water for 1 minute, then transfer to the water bath. When the onions are cool, peel them.

3. Place all the vegetables, including the blanched onions, in the center of a large square of doubled-up cheesecloth and tie in a tight bundle. Add the bundle to the stockpot and simmer for 8 minutes. Add the chorizo and simmer 3 more minutes, periodically skimming the surface of the soup. Remove the bundle, cut it open, and transfer the vegetables to the platter Shred the chicken.

4. Strain the broth, then add the parsley.

5. Ladle the broth into cups or small bowls and serve with the vegetables and chicken with the mustard on the side.

15

sancocho paisa
[countrymen's stew]

Sancocho is a peasant-style dish—you throw everything in the pot and boil it. *Paisa* (pie-EE-saw) is slang, meaning "like a brother," as in "Hey, brother, how are you doing?" This dish is usually made with beef or pork ribs, but I use both because I like the added flavor. It's one of the best soups for cold, lazy winter days because it's easy to make and the saffron will fill your house with a rich, earthy aroma as the soup cooks.

SERVES 6 TO 8

1 gallon beef stock (page 115)

1 pound boneless shortribs, trimmed

1 pound pork ribs, cut into 2-inch pieces

1 teaspoon ground cumin

1 tablespoon saffron threads

1 teaspoon salt

1 teaspoon freshly ground black pepper

2 green plantains, with skin, cut crosswise into $^1/_2$-inch slices

$^1/_2$ pound yuca, peeled, cored, and cut into large dice

2 large russet potatoes, peeled

1 large plus 2 small carrots, grated

4 large leeks, white parts only

$^1/_2$ large (6 ounces) green cabbage, julienned

2 ears sweet corn, cut crosswise into 1-inch pinwheels

2 ripe plantains, with black skin, cut crosswise into $^1/_2$-inch-thick slices

4 green onions, white and green parts sliced crosswise

3 sprigs cilantro, leaves removed and stems discarded

3 sprigs parsley, leaves removed and stems discarded

1. In a large stockpot over high heat, bring the stock, ribs, cumin, saffron, salt, and pepper to a boil. Decrease the heat to low, cover, and simmer for 45 minutes.

2. Bring a large saucepan of water to a boil. Add the green plantains and boil for 10 minutes, then drain.

3. Add the plantains, yuca, potatoes, carrots, leeks, cabbage, and corn to the stockpot. Cook for 15 minutes. Using a large wire mesh strainer, remove the meat and vegetables from the stockpot. Arrange on a large platter.

4. Ladle the broth into bowls and serve with the ripe plantain slices, green onions, cilantro, parsley, cooked plantains, yuca, potatoes, carrots, leeks, cabbage, and corn on the side. Garnish the broth with the green onions and cilantro and parsley leaves, then sip it as you alternately eat the ribs and vegetables.

conejo con coco
[rabbit cooked in coconut milk]

This is my interpretation of a popular dish from coastal Colombia. Colombians don't put ginger or serrano chiles in theirs, but I think the flavor of coconut milk is enhanced by the spiciness of chiles and the sharpness of the ginger. Colombians add rum and freshly grated coconut, which complement the richness of the coconut milk and rabbit, but I prefer a stew with more contrast. You'll find this one on the menu at Patria, where it's always been popular. When you buy the rabbit, ask the butcher to cut it into 16 pieces, splitting each leg and quartering the loins.

SERVES 4

1 cup flour

$^1/_2$ teaspoon salt

1 scant teaspoon freshly ground black pepper

1 whole skinned rabbit, cut up

$^1/_4$ cup olive oil

1 white onion, diced

6 cloves garlic, pounded into a paste

4 ounces fresh ginger, peeled and grated

2 red bell peppers, diced

1 cup dark rum

1 12-ounce can coconut milk

3 serrano chiles, stemmed, seeded, deribbed, and sliced

2 cups chicken stock (page 116)

8 plum tomatoes, diced

1 cup freshly grated or unsweetened, dry coconut

1 lime, quartered

1. Combine the flour, salt, and pepper in a mixing bowl. Add the rabbit pieces and toss to coat evenly.

2. Heat the oil in a large skillet over high heat and brown the rabbit on all sides. Add the onion, garlic, ginger, and bell peppers, and stir. Cook about 10 minutes. Carefully add the rum, then decrease the heat to low. Add the coconut milk, chiles, and stock. Cover and simmer for 35 minutes.

3. Uncover the stockpot, add the tomatoes, stir, and cook for 10 minutes.

4. Stir the soup, then ladle it into bowls. Sprinkle some of the coconut over each bowl and serve with the lime wedges on the side. Squeeze lime juice over soup before eating.

seco de chivo
[goat stew]

Seco means "dry," *chivo* means "goat." This is a wonderful, classic Peruvian stew that's not very wet. A lot of people aren't familiar with goat meat and are reluctant to cook with it, but I happen to be a big fan of it. Goats are close relatives of lamb, but taste less gamy, almost like a cross between lamb and white veal. Goat isn't that easy to find, but you may be able to get it from a good butcher in Latin neighborhoods. Whenever I have a chance to order goat meat for Patria or Aguarela, I buy two and get about ten or fifteen portions out of each one. That's enough to make this stew with the leg meat and grill the loin. When you serve seco, you have to serve it the way they do in Peru, with three things on the side: rice, boiled potatoes, and fried yuca strips, all of which contribute a different texture to the meal. Peru is the only country in the world where you can serve three starches with something and get away with it. I've added two ingredients to the stew, Peruvian *chicha de jora* (corn beer) and ketchup, which increase its depth of flavor. If you can't find chicha de jora, you can substitute 4 parts beer and 1 part apple cider. Chicha de jora mixed with a little ketchup is my favorite sauce in the whole world. Try it.

SERVES 8 TO 10

1/2 cup achiote oil (page 115)

1 goat leg (about 4 pounds), cut into 1 x 1-inch dice

4 large onions, finely diced

20 cloves garlic, diced

5 jalapeño chiles, stemmed and diced (including seeds)

1 teaspoon ground cumin

1 teaspoon ground allspice

1 teaspoon dried coriander

6 plum tomatoes, diced

6 cups chicha de jora (corn beer), or 4 cups beer and 1 cup apple cider

6 ancho chiles, stemmed and seeded

2 ají amarillo peppers, stemmed and seeded

4 cups water

4 large russet potatoes, peeled and finely diced

6 ounces ketchup

2 ounces Worcestershire sauce

3 ounces crushed red pepper flakes

2 ounces distilled white vinegar

Salt and freshly ground black pepper

10 sprigs cilantro leaves

1. Heat the achiote oil in a large stockpot over very high heat. Add the goat meat and brown, cooking about 6 minutes while stirring. Add the onions and garlic and cook 5 more minutes. Stir in the jalapeños, cumin, allspice, coriander, and tomatoes.

2. In a blender, combine 2 cups of the chicha de jora and the ancho and ají amarillo peppers. Let sit 5 minutes (to soften the chiles), then blend on high until puréed.

3. Add the blended chile mixture, the goat mixture, the remaining 4 cups chicha de jora, and the water to the stockpot. Bring to a boil, then decrease the heat to low, cover, and simmer for 1 hour and 20 minutes. Stir the stew two or three times while it cooks, checking to make sure it's cooking down and thickening.

4. When the meat starts to become tender, add the potatoes, ketchup, Worcestershire, pepper flakes, and vinegar. Cook 10 more minutes. Season to taste with salt and pepper. Cook 5 more minutes, then turn off the heat and let rest 10 minutes (still covered).

5. Coarsely chop the cilantro leaves. Ladle the soup into bowls, sprinkle with cilantro, and serve.

sopa de carne y cebada
[beef and barley soup]

This isn't your standard beef and barley soup because it's flavored with corn beer. (*Chicha* means "fermented drink" and *jora* is usually blue corn.) If you can't find corn beer at your local Latin market, just substitute 12 ounces of ale combined with 4 ounces of apple cider. That will more or less give you the flavor of chicha de jora. Adding fresh basil right at the end really brings out the flavors of the barley and the meat. Enjoy it.

SERVES 4

2 tablespoons sweet butter

1 teaspoon ground allspice

1 tablespoon dried oregano

1 pound skirt steak, cut into small cubes

1 white onion, diced

4 cloves garlic, diced

3 jalapeño chiles, stemmed and diced (including seeds)

2 stalks celery, diced

1 carrot, peeled and diced

16 ounces chicha de jora (corn beer), or 12 ounces ale and 4 ounces apple cider

1 gallon corn stock (page 116)

2 tablespoons tomato paste

3 plum tomatoes, diced

1 cup barley

4 ears sweet white corn, shucked and kernels sliced off cobs

Salt

6 sprigs basil, leaves julienned

1. Heat the butter in a large stockpot over medium-high heat. Stir in the allspice and oregano. Increase the heat to high. Immediately add the steak and brown on all sides, about 12 minutes.

2. Add the onion, garlic, jalapeños, celery, and carrot to the stockpot and sauté about 5 minutes. Add the chicha de jora and reduce to half the original volume, about 7 minutes. Add the stock, increase the heat to high and bring to a boil. When boiling, add the tomato paste and tomatoes and stir well to dissolve the paste. Add the barley and corn, and bring to a boil again. Decrease the heat to low, cover, and simmer for 45 minutes. Season to taste with salt.

3. Ladle the soup into bowls. Sprinkle some of the basil over each bowl and serve.

sopa de carne guarani
[white rice and ground beef soup]

The name of this soup comes from the language of the indigenous people of Paraguay. The ground beef looks a bit like hash simmering in broth—it's a good home-style soup.

SERVES 4

$^1/_2$ cup long-grain white rice

$^1/_2$ cup hot water

1 pound ground beef

$^1/_2$ teaspoon salt

$^1/_2$ teaspoon freshly ground black pepper

$^1/_2$ cup plus 3 tablespoons olive oil

2 ears sweet yellow corn, kernels cut off cobs

6 green onions, white and green parts

1 white onion, diced

1 tablespoon pulverized garlic (with mortar and pestle)

6 plum tomatoes

3 quarts strong beef stock (page 115)

1 tablespoon dried oregano

salt and freshly ground black pepper

$^1/_2$ cup chopped flat-leaf parsley leaves

Unseasoned croutons

1. Soak the rice in the hot water for 10 minutes. Drain the rice and transfer to a blender. Purée until almost liquified, about 1 minute.

2. Using your hands, combine the meat and puréed rice. Add the salt and pepper and mix until evenly incorporated.

3. Place 3 tablespoons of the oil, the corn, green onions, white onion, garlic, and tomatoes in the bowl of a food processor and pulse until finely puréed.

4. Heat the $^1/_2$ cup of oil in a large stockpot over high heat. Add the puréed vegetable mixture and cook about 10 minutes, stirring often. Add the stock and bring to a boil. Add the oregano and season to taste with salt and pepper. Decrease the heat to low and simmer for 1 hour.

5. Stir in the parsley. Ladle the soup into bowls, float some of the croutons on top, and serve.

BORi-BORi
[RicH BROTH WiTH dumpLiNGS, CORN, aNd SHORTRiBS]

For this soup, I went crazy playing with a classic Paraguayan recipe. I make my dumplings out of masa harina (which Paraguayans don't actually use), yellow cornmeal, and Parmesan to get a dry corn taste without grittiness and a smoother, richer flavor. The dumplings cook in beef stock, along with the braised shortribs. This is definitely a meal in itself. You can use chicken stock if you prefer, or cook the dumplings in another soup altogether. The recipe is foolproof, so you can be sure it will come out right the first time you make it. I've also added a cinnamon stick and dry sherry to give it just a little sweetness and a slight lift.

SERVES 4 TO 6

1 cup very fine yellow cornmeal

$1/2$ cup masa harina

1 cup grated Parmesan cheese

2 teaspoons salt

8 green onions, sliced

*2 ears corn, shucked and kernels
    cut off cobs*

2 tablespoons sweet butter, softened

2 eggs

1 tablespoon sugar

1 gallon beef stock (page 115)

2 bay leaves

2 whole cloves

1 cinnamon stick

*1 pound boneless beef shortribs,
    cut into 1-inch cubes*

*4 sprigs flat-leaf parsley, leaves
    coarsely chopped*

1 cup dry sherry

Chives, cut into 2-inch lengths

1. In a mixing bowl, combine the cornmeal, masa harina, Parmesan, and 1 teaspoon of the salt; mix well and set aside.

2. Place all but 2 tablespoons of the green onions, corn kernels, butter, eggs, sugar, and the remaining teaspoon of salt in the bowl of a food processor. Pulse about 1 minute, or until finely puréed.

3. Using your hands, work the puréed corn mixture into the dry ingredients. Knead until well incorporated. Let the mixture rest 10 minutes. Knead again for 3 minutes, then form it into small balls (about 20 pieces). Roll each ball between your palms to make it nicely rounded.

4. In a medium stockpot over high heat, bring 1 gallon of water to a boil, then lower the heat to medium-low, and let the water slow to a rolling simmer. Line a tray with waxed paper. Place the dumplings in the water and cook 10 minutes. (Cook in batches if necessary.) Using a skimmer, transfer the cooked dumplings to the tray.

5. In a large stockpot over high heat, combine the stock, bay leaves, cloves, and cinnamon and bring to a boil. When boiling, decrease the heat to low, cover, and simmer for about 20 minutes.

6. Add the beef, remaining green onions, parsley, sherry, and chives and simmer for 10 more minutes. Add the dumplings and simmer for 1 minute, then ladle into bowls and serve.

buseca
[garbanzo bean and tripe soup]

Many cooks in the States are turned off by tripe's strong aroma. Don't be one of them! Its chewy texture is satisfying, and its pungency is practically washed away when it is cleaned properly (see below).

SERVES 6 TO 8

1 pound honeycomb tripe

6 cups ice water

1 cup plus 2 tablespoons distilled white vinegar

5 bay leaves

1 tablespoon red pepper flakes

1 tablespoon dried thyme

1 tablespoon dried oregano

1 gallon water

$^1/_4$ cup olive oil

2 white onions, diced

4 plum tomatoes, diced

6 cloves garlic, minced

$^1/_4$ cup chopped parsley leaves

2 bay leaves

1 gallon beef stock (page 115)

$^1/_2$ cup dried garbanzo beans, soaked in water overnight and drained

1 cup dried white navy beans

2 turnips, peeled and diced

4 carrots, peeled and cut into $^1/_4$-inch-thick rounds

$^1/_2$ head white cabbage, shredded

1 cup long-grain white rice, rinsed well

12 ounces chorizo sausage (about 3)

12 ounces morcilla sausage (about 3)

1 cup grated queso blanco or other queso fresco

5 sprigs basil leaves, julienned

1. Thoroughly rinse the tripe under cold running water. Fill a large bowl with the ice water and add 2 tablespoons of the vinegar. Place the tripe in the bowl and let soak for 30 minutes. Remove from the water, pat dry, and cut into 1-inch cubes.

2. In a large stockpot, combine the tripe, bay leaves, pepper flakes, thyme, oregano, water, and the remaining 1 cup of vinegar. Bring to a boil over high heat and cook at a full boil for 1 hour. Remove from the heat and let cool. Drain tripe, rinse in cold water, and reserve.

3. In another large stockpot over high heat, combine the oil, onions, tomatoes, garlic, parsley, and bay leaves. Stir and cook for 5 minutes. Add the stock, reserved tripe, garbanzos, white beans, and turnips, and bring to a boil. Decrease the heat, cover, and simmer for 1 hour.

4. Add the carrots, cabbage, and rice. Re-cover and simmer for another hour. Add the chorizo, morcilla, cheese, and basil. Stir and simmer for 10 minutes.

5. Ladle the soup into bowls and serve.

sopa de maní y cordero
[peanut and lamb soup]

Peanuts are commonly used in Bolivian cuisine, as in Brazilian food, but in land-locked Bolivia they are more likely to be paired with meat or river fish than seafood. And the meats of choice would be guinea pig, or most probably lamb, but rarely beef, which is at a premium in Latin America.

SERVES 4 TO 6

2 large lamb shanks, fat trimmed off
2 bay leaves
1 teaspoon crushed red pepper flakes
3 sprigs thyme
6 cloves garlic, minced
1 teaspoon ground allspice
1 gallon plus 3 cups water
3 tablespoons peanut oil
1 white onion, diced
1 red bell pepper, diced
2 jalapeño chiles, stemmed and diced (including seeds)
4 plum tomatoes, diced
2 cups dry-roasted, unsalted peanuts
1 green plantain, peeled and diced
¹/₄ cup smooth peanut butter
6 green onions, white and green parts finely sliced
6 sprigs mint

1. In a large stockpot, combine the lamb shanks, bay leaves, pepper flakes, thyme, garlic, allspice, and 1 gallon of the water. Gradually bring to a boil over medium-low heat, then decrease heat to low, cover and simmer for about $2^1/_2$ hours.

2. Uncover the stockpot, turn off the heat, and let the shanks cool completely in the stock, about 2 hours.

3. Strain the stock, reserving the liquid and meat in separate containers and discarding the bay leaves and thyme.

4. Heat the oil in another large stockpot over high heat. Add the onion, bell pepper, jalapeños, and tomatoes, and sauté for about 10 minutes. Add the peanuts, plantain, reserved stock, and remaining 3 cups of water, and bring to a boil. Decrease the heat to low, cover, and simmer for 1 hour. Meanwhile, using two forks, shred the lamb.

5. Uncover the stockpot and add the peanut butter and green onions. Purée the soup with handheld blender. Stir in the lamb.

6. Ladle the soup into bowls. Garnish each bowl with a few mint leaves and serve.

carbonada criolla
[traditional meat stew]

I tell you, when I first read about this classic Argentinian recipe, I never believed that peaches and squash would be a good combination. But when I tried the soup, with the addition of all the other ingredients, especially the cumin and touch of balsamic vinegar, it had an unbelievable flavor. I can't explain exactly why it's so good—you'll just have to try it yourself and see what I mean.

SERVES 6 TO 8

1 large (7- to 8-pound) calabaza
$1/4$ cup flour
1 tablespoon Hungarian paprika
1 teaspoon chipotle chile powder
1 teaspoon ground white pepper
1 tablespoon salt
1 tablespoon dried oregano
3 pounds boneless beef shortribs, cut into 1-inch-wide strips
$1/4$ cup olive oil
4 fresh peaches, peeled and sliced
2 tablespoons sugar
$1/4$ cup balsamic vinegar
1 white onion, diced
5 cloves garlic
3 stalks celery, diced
1 gallon beef stock (page 115)
2 bay leaves
1 teaspoon ground cumin

2 ears sweet corn, shucked and cut into $1/2$-inch-thick pinwheels
2 carrots, peeled and cut into thin rounds

1. With a damp cloth, clean the outside of the calabaza. With a sharp paring knife, about 3 inches from the stem, cut around the stem and lift off the "lid." Using a large metal spoon, scoop out the seeds. Next, scoop out the flesh, being careful to leave about $1/4$ to $1/2$ inch of flesh all around the inside. Cut flesh into $1/2$-inch pieces.

2. In a mixing bowl, combine the flour, paprika, chile powder, white pepper, salt, and oregano. Add the shortribs and toss to coat evenly.

3. Preheat the oven to 350°. Brush the inside of the calabaza and the underside of the lid with 2 tablespoons of the oil. Set the calabaza and lid, flesh side up, in a deep roasting pan and bake for 15 minutes. Let cool.

4. In another mixing bowl, toss the peach slices with the balsamic vinegar. Set aside.

5. Heat the remaining 2 tablespoons of oil in a stockpot over high heat. Add the shortribs and brown well on all sides, about 12 minutes. Add the onion, garlic,

and celery, and cook for 5 more minutes. Add the stock, bay leaves, and cumin and bring to a boil. Decrease the heat to low, cover, and simmer for about $1^1/_2$ hours.

6. Uncover the stockpot and add the corn and carrots. Increase the heat to high and bring the soup back to a full boil. Boil for 10 minutes, then add the cal-abaza and peaches. Stir and cook for 10 more minutes.

7. Carefully ladle the soup into the calabaza shell. Cook with lid on in the oven for 30 minutes.

8. At the table, remove the calabaza lid, then ladle the hot soup out of the pumpkin into bowls and serve.

ají de gallina
[chile and chicken stew]

Ají means "chile" in Peru and *gallina* is
the spanish word commonly used for
"hen." This chile and chicken stew is one
of the primary dishes of traditional
Peruvian cuisine. I've eaten a lot of different versions and asked every Peruvian
I've met if they have a good recipe for it.
My recipe is adapted from Felipe Rojas-
Lombardi's, which appeared in his book
The Art of South American Cooking.
It's the best I've ever had. I've cooked it
over a hundred times, and it always
turns out perfect. Lombardi added lime
and orange juice to his dish, which I love
because they give it real zing. Even
though I never met Felipe Rojas-
Lombardi, his work has provided constant inspiration for me.

SERVES 6 TO 8

1 large whole chicken, including neck
  (about 3 pounds)
1 white onion, cut into large dice
2 tablespoons small carrots, peeled
  and cut crosswise into 2-inch slices
3 stalks celery, chopped
Several sprigs fresh thyme
Several sprigs fresh dill
Several sprigs fresh parsley
3 bay leaves
1 tablespoon black peppercorns
1 teaspoon crushed red pepper flakes
1 tablespoon salt
4 quarts water
1 cup freshly squeezed orange juice
$1/4$ cup freshly squeezed lime juice
5 marisol chiles
$1/2$ cup (8 ounces) sweet butter
3 to 4 white onions, diced
  (about 4 cups)
1 teaspoon turmeric
4 slices white bread
1 12.5-ounce can evaporated milk
1 cup walnuts, finely chopped
10 small new potatoes, boiled
  and peeled
2 tablespoons crumbled feta cheese
2 hard-boiled eggs, thinly sliced
8 to 10 pitted kalamata olives, sliced

1. In a large stockpot, bring the chicken, neck, onion, carrots, celery, thyme, dill, parsley, bay leaves, peppercorns, pepper flakes, salt, and water to a boil. Decrease the heat to low and simmer for 50 minutes, or until the chicken is tender. Remove the chicken from the stockpot and set aside to cool.

2. Continue to cook the stock for 15 minutes, then strain into a clean stockpot and set aside.

3. Using two forks, shred the chicken. Remove any meat clinging to the chicken bones.

4. In a small mixing bowl, combine the orange and lime juices. Crumble or break the chiles into pieces and soak them in the juice for 20 minutes. Transfer to a blender and blend until smooth. Set aside.

5. In a large sauté pan over medium heat, melt the butter. Add the onions and turmeric and cook until onions are translucent, about 8 minutes.

6. Soak the bread in the evaporated milk.

7. Add the blended chile mixture to the sauté pan and continue cooking until the liquid cooks off, about 10 minutes. Meanwhile, skim off any fat and impurities that may have risen to the surface of the cooling stock.

8. Add the soaked bread (discarding the evaporated milk) to the sauté pan and cook for about 30 seconds, stirring continuously. Add the blended pepper mixture to the stock. Add the walnuts, potatoes, and feta. Cook about 30 minutes, stirring occasionally, or until thick enough to coat the spoon. Add the chicken meat and simmer 10 minutes.

9. Ladle the stew into bowls. Float some of the egg and olive slices on the surface of the soup in each bowl, then serve.

CONCH GUISADO DE RAMÓN MADRANO

GUISO DE MOLONDRONES Y CAMARONES

SOPA DE ALMEJAS CON PATACONES

SOPA DE CARACOL

CHILE DE CONCHAS

PANAMANIAN CALDILLO

SOPA DE TIBURÓN

BACALAO A LA NICA

ENCEBOLLADO DE ATÚN

GUISO DE MAÍZ CON CANGREJO

FANESCA

BICHE MANABITA

fish- and seafood-based soups

harina con cangrejo

chipi chipi

fosforito margariteño

choros

chupe de marisco

chupe de camarones

vatapá

sopa galopín de mar

moqueca

zarzuela de mariscos

conch guisado de ramón madrano
[ramón madrano's conch stew]

Fresh conch is plentiful in Santo Domingo, but nearly impossible to find in the States. I think it loses a lot of its texture when frozen, so do your best to use fresh in this recipe. This is a great chili-like dish created by my friend and previous employee Ramón Madrano, whose native country is Santo Domingo. He is an expert at cooking conch and would make delicious things with it whenever some came in at the restaurant. This was one of his best dishes. The secret is the rum, which brings out the sweetness of the conch and adds a whole other dimension to the dish.

SERVES 4

> 3 tablespoons lard
> 2 pounds conch meat, cleaned
>   and diced
> 1 white onion, diced
> 5 cloves garlic, crushed
> 3 bay leaves, crushed
> 1 tablespoon oregano
> 6 plum tomatoes, diced
> 2 potatoes, peeled and diced
> 1 teaspoon dried thyme
> 4 jalapeño chiles, stemmed and diced
>   (including seeds)
> 1 teaspoon ground cayenne pepper
> 1 cup dark rum
> 3 quarts fish stock (page 117)
> 10 sprigs cilantro
> 1 red bell pepper, diced
> 1 yellow bell pepper, diced
> 2 tablespoons flat-leaf parsley

1. Heat the lard in a heavy-bottomed stockpot over high heat. Add the conch and cook, stirring continuously, about 4 minutes. Add the onion, garlic, bay leaves, oregano, tomatoes, potatoes, thyme, jalapeños, and cayenne and cook about 5 minutes.

2. Add the rum and let the alcohol cook out, stirring continuously, about 2 minutes. Add the stock and bring the mixture to a boil.

3. When the soup is boiling, decrease the heat to low and simmer for 25 to 30 minutes.

4. Remove the cilantro leaves from the stems, discard the stems, and coarsely chop the leaves. Add the bell peppers and cook about 5 more minutes, then stir in the cilantro and parsley.

5. Ladle the stew into bowls and serve immediately.

guiso de molondrones y camarones
[okra and shrimp stew]

Molondrón is the Dominican word for okra, which is one ingredient that every Latin American country has a different name for. The list of all the names is too long to give here, but *molondrón* and *quimbombó* are a couple of my favorites. Although okra is popular in Latin America, it is not an indigenous vegetable. African slaves brought it to the New World, and it traveled south over the years. Presoaking and rinsing the okra washes away its naturally slimy quality.

SERVES 4

$1/4$ cup freshly squeezed lemon juice

1 quart water

2 cups okra, ends and caps removed, cut into 1-inch slices

3 tablespoons olive oil

$1/4$ cup achiote oil (page 115)

1 white onion, peeled and diced

1 red bell pepper, diced

1 green bell pepper, diced

4 cloves garlic, diced

3 quarts shrimp stock (page 119)

3 bay leaves

1 tablespoon dried oregano

6 plum tomatoes, diced

2 tablespoons tomato paste

$1^1/2$ pounds medium shrimp, peeled and deveined

1 teaspoon ground cumin

1 tablespoon ground chile powder

1 Scotch bonnet chile pepper, seeded and diced small

Salt and freshly ground black pepper

2 cups cooked long-grain white rice (page 114)

1. In a mixing bowl, combine the lemon juice and water. Add the okra and soak for 30 minutes. Transfer the okra to a colander and rinse under running water for 20 minutes.

2. Heat the olive oil and achiote oil in a large, heavy-bottomed stockpot over high heat. Add the onion, bell peppers, and garlic, and cook about 5 minutes.

3. Add the shrimp stock, bay leaves, oregano, tomatoes, tomato paste, shrimp, cumin, chile powder, and chile pepper. Bring the mixture to a boil, then decrease the heat to low and cook about 15 minutes. Season to taste with salt and pepper.

4. Divide the rice among the bowls, then ladle the stew over it and serve.

sopa de almejas con patacones
[clam soup with plantains]

Just reading the recipe makes me hungry for a bowlful of this soup, with its salty clams and nutty fried plantains, all washed down with a glass of good dry white wine. *Patacones* means different things in different countries. In Panama, where I got the idea for this soup, it refers to green plantains. You may add the cooked clams to the soup while still in their shells, but I prefer to remove the clam meat and discard the shells because the plantains make the soup really thick and the shells just get in the way. If you prefer, you may substitute canned chopped clams and bottled clam juice.

SERVES 4 TO 6

SOUP

5 pounds cherrystone clams, shells well scrubbed, or 2 pounds cooked clams, shells discarded and juice reserved

2 quarts milk

3 quarts water

2 bay leaves

1 teaspoon black peppercorns

1 tablespoon distilled white vinegar

8 ounces bacon, diced

1 white onion, diced

5 cloves garlic, crushed

3 tablespoons all-purpose flour

2 cups heavy cream

FRIED PLANTAINS

1 cup vegetable oil

2 green plantains, peeled and cut into 1-inch pieces

Salt

———

1 to 2 limes, quartered

1. If using clams in shells, place in large mixing bowl and cover with the milk. Soak for 30 minutes, then drain and reserve.

2. In a large stockpot, bring 1 quart of the water, the bay leaves, peppercorns, and vinegar to a boil. Add half of the clams in shells and cover. Let boil and cook about 5 minutes, regularly shaking the pot. Remove the clams from the pot with a long-handled strainer, transferring them to a free-standing strainer to cool. Repeat with the remaining clams. When cool, pick the clam meat out of the shells, discarding the shells. Strain the broth through a fine-meshed strainer lined with cheesecloth. Reserve the broth and clams.

3. In a large stockpot over high heat, render the bacon until crispy around the edges, about 5 minutes. Add the onion and garlic and cook about 3 minutes. Stir in the flour and cook 2 more minutes, stirring continuously. Add the reserved clam broth, the remaining 2 quarts water, and the cooked clams. Bring to a boil, then decrease the heat and simmer for 10 minutes. Add heavy cream and simmer another 10 minutes.

4. In a large, heavy-bottomed skillet, heat the oil to 250°. Drop half of the plantains into the oil and fry about 7 minutes per side. Remove with a wire-mesh strainer and set on paper towels to drain. Repeat with the remaining plantain pieces. Using the back of a spoon or a sturdy spatula, mash down the plantain pieces until $1/2$ inch thick. Increase the heat to high and bring temperature of the oil to 375°. Refry the plantains until golden brown, sprinkling them with salt immediately after removing them from the oil.

5. Add plantains to soup just before serving. Ladle into bowls and serve with the lime wedges. Squeeze lime juice over the soup before eating.

sopa de caracol
[conch soup]

Caracol means "conch" in Spanish, and this conch soup is my interpretation of one of Honduras's most popular dishes. The soup is so popular in Honduras that there was a hit song about it that ran for three years or so. I don't know who sang it, but it was called Sopa de Caracol, and they actually invented a dance to go with it that was as popular as the macarena— an actual dance for Sopa de Caracol! I've eaten this dish a lot, and kept it on the menu at Patria for a long time. It's one of the best soups in my repertoire. Coconut and conch are just a classic combination that I use not only in other soups, but in several entirely different dishes, like my coconut-conch rice and conch fritters with coconut sauce. If you can't find fresh conch, frozen will be just as good.

SERVES 4

2 tablespoons olive oil

1 pound conch, coarsely ground

1 white onion, diced

1 teaspoon minced garlic

1 ounce fresh ginger, peeled and grated

4 jalapeño chiles, stemmed and diced (including seeds)

3 quarts fish stock (page 117)

1 14-ounce can coconut milk

1 carrot, peeled and diced

2 stalks celery, diced

1 red bell pepper, diced

1 pound yuca, halved lengthwise

4 plum tomatoes, diced

Salt and freshly ground black pepper

1/4 cup cilantro leaves

1 chive, sliced

1 green onion, white and green parts sliced

Unsweetened shredded coconut

1 lime, quartered

1. Heat the olive oil in a large stockpot over high heat. Add the conch, onion, garlic, ginger, and jalapeños and briefly sauté, about 5 minutes. Add the stock and coconut milk, and bring to a boil. Add the carrot, celery, bell pepper, and yuca. Cover and continue to boil for 5 minutes. Decrease the heat and simmer for 30 minutes.

2. Uncover the soup, add the tomatoes and and season to taste with salt and pepper. Cook 10 more minutes, stirring continuously.

3. Just before serving, stir in the cilantro, chive, and green onion.

4. Ladle the soup into bowls. Sprinkle coconut over the top and serve with the lime wedges on the side. Squeeze lime juice over the soup before eating.

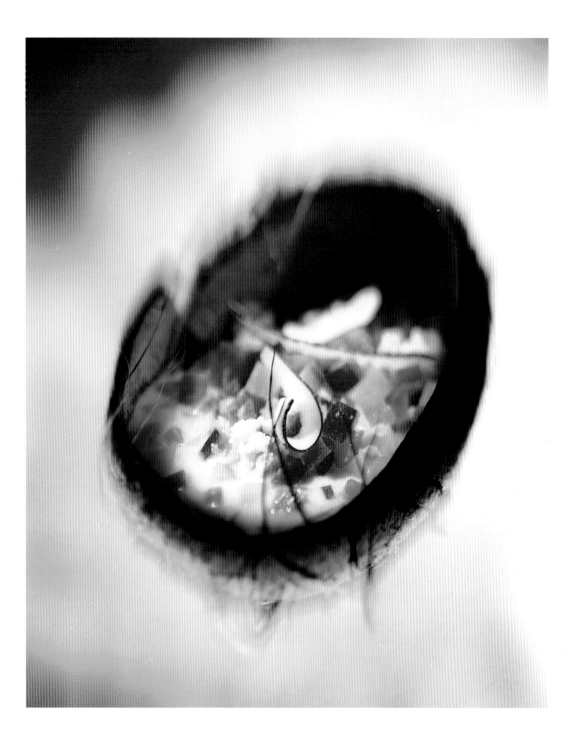

chile de conchas
[scallop chili]

One of the cooks at Patria created this recipe. The lobster stock gives it a nice rich flavor, and the tiny sea scallops create great "mouth feel." But don't jump the gun and add the scallops early because they only need to sit in the hot stew for a few minutes to come out perfectly cooked. The squeeze of lime juice at the end lifts all the flavors.

SERVES 6

10 ounces dried pinto beans
1 gallon lobster stock (page 117)
2 bay leaves
3 tablespoons achiote oil (page 115)
1 white onion, diced
1 red bell pepper, diced
1 green bell pepper, diced
4 jalapeño chiles, stemmed and diced (including seeds)
4 cloves garlic, diced
8 plum tomatoes, diced
6 ounces calabaza, diced (about $1/2$ cup)
1 tablespoon ground ancho chile powder
1 teaspoon ground chipotle chile powder
1 teaspoon ground cumin
1 teaspoon salt
1 pound small sea scallops, gently rinsed and patted dry

1 bunch green onions, white and green parts sliced
1 bunch chives
$1/2$ cup cilantro leaves
1 lime, quartered

1. In a large stockpot over low heat, bring the beans, stock, and bay leaves to a slow, rolling simmer. Cover and let cook 45 minutes, then uncover and continue to simmer.

2. While the beans are cooking, heat the achiote oil in a sauté pan over medium heat. Add the onion, bell peppers, jalapeños, and garlic to the pan and sauté, stirring often, for 6 to 8 minutes or until the onion is transparent. Add the sauté mixture to the stockpot.

3. Add the tomatoes, calabaza, chile powders, cumin, and salt to the stockpot and simmer for 30 more minutes.

4. Taste the stew and adjust the seasoning, if necessary. Add the scallops and cover. Remove the stew from the heat and let sit, still covered, 10 minutes.

5. Uncover and add the green onions, chives, and cilantro. Ladle the chili into bowls and serve with the lime wedges on the side. Squeeze lime juice over the stew before eating.

caldillo desde panama
[panamanian broth with seafood and tomatoes]

Caldillo is a spanish word for "broth." I learned to make this soup from the mother of one of my employees at Yuca. She insisted on making it for me one Sunday, and sent it in with her son when he came to work. We reheated and tasted it, and I fell in love with it immediately. The combination of oregano and tomatoes is classic—the oregano brings out their flavor like no other spice can.

SERVES 4 TO 6

¹/₄ cup olive oil

2 white onions, diced

1 green bell pepper, diced

2 poblano chiles, diced

6 cloves garlic, crushed

10 very ripe beefsteak tomatoes, chopped

2 tablespoons tomato paste

3 quarts shrimp stock (page 119)

2 tablespoons fresh oregano leaves

1 teaspoon cumin

4 eggs, well beaten

1 pound jumbo lump crabmeat

1 pound rock shrimp, peeled

Salt and freshly ground black pepper to taste

1. In a large stockpot, heat the olive oil over high heat and sauté the onions, bell pepper, poblanos, and garlic about 5 minutes, stirring often. Add the tomatoes and cook another 5 minutes.

2. Add the tomato paste and stock, then bring to a boil, stirring often. Let boil 5 minutes. Add the oregano and cumin and stir.

3. Working quickly, while the soup is boiling, add the eggs in a fine stream, then reduce to a simmer. Stir, then let cook 10 more minutes. Add the crab and shrimp. Cover and remove from the heat. Let sit 5 to 7 minutes before serving.

4. Stir the soup well, then ladle into bowls and serve.

39

sopa de tiburón
[shark soup]

Efrain Veiga, my partner when I was at Yuca in Miami, learned how to make this soup while he lived in Costa Rica, where he tried to start a salt-cured shark business, as is usually done with cod. Mako shark, which is like swordfish but drier, is the best shark to use for this—because of its flavor and its reputation as an aphrodisiac in Latin America. The original recipe called for standard green beans, but I use haricots verts to make the soup more elegant. It has a light broth base, but it's very "meaty."

SERVES 4 TO 6

1 gallon fish stock (page 117)

4 bay leaves

3 sprigs thyme

1 pound mako shark loin, cubed

5 plum tomatoes, peeled, seeded, and diced (page 121)

2 red bell peppers, roasted, seeded, and diced with skin on (page 121)

2 cloves garlic

1 750-ml bottle dry white wine

$^{1}/_{2}$ pound haricots verts

1 small red onion, thinly sliced

Salt and freshly ground black pepper

1 lime, quartered

1. In a large stockpot over high heat, bring the stock, bay leaves, and thyme to a boil. Add the shark, decrease the heat to low, cover and simmer for 20 minutes. Remove the shark with a strainer and set aside to cool. Add the tomatoes, bell peppers, garlic, and wine to the stockpot and continue to simmer.

2. When the shark is cool, flake the cubes with a fork.

3. Add the green beans and red onion to the soup. Just before serving, add the shark and season to taste with salt and pepper.

4. Ladle the soup into bowls and serve with the lime wedges on the side. Squeeze lime juice over the soup before eating.

Bacalao a La Nica
[Nicaraguan salted cod soup]

This is a classical Nicaraguan dish. Bacalao is codfish cured with salt, and anybody from Nicaragua is known as a *nica.* I think the raisins are what make it so interesting. The saltiness of the bacalao and the sweetness of the raisins in every other bite creates a soup that's a lot of fun to eat.

SERVES 4

1 pound bacalao, boneless and skinless

2 quarts water

2 bay leaves

2 tablespoons olive oil

1 white onion, diced

3 cloves garlic, minced

8 plum tomatoes, diced

2 potatoes, finely diced

²/₃ cup evaporated milk

1 cup water

6 ounces Parmesan cheese, grated

4 ounces raisins

1 green onion, green parts only, sliced

1 red bell pepper, diced

1. In a saucepan over medium heat, bring the bacalao, water, and bay leaves to a gentle boil and cook 45 minutes. Remove the fish from the stock and set in a strainer to cool.

2. When the fish is cool, flake it with a fork.

3. Heat the oil in a sauté pan over medium heat. Add the onion and sauté 3 minutes. Add the garlic and tomatoes and sauté 10 more minutes. Add the flaked bacalao, potatoes, evaporated milk, and 1 cup water. Bring to a boil and stir in the Parmesan. Decrease the heat, cover, and let simmer for 15 minutes.

4. Uncover the stockpot, add the raisins, and stir. Cook 3 more minutes.

5. Ladle the soup into bowls. Sprinkle some of the green onion and bell pepper over each bowl and serve.

encebollado de atún
[onioned tuna soup]

I first tasted this soup at La Canoa, a restaurant in Guayaquil, Ecuador. They prepared the tuna in the popular style of leaving it mostly rare, then they added it to the soup right before serving. When we serve the soup at the restaurant, we use all the meaty trimmings from the tuna steaks we've served as full portions.

SERVES 6

1 pound yuca, peeled, cored, and cut into 1¹/₂- to 2-inch lengths

3 tablespoons olive oil

1 white onion, diced (about 1 cup)

4 plum tomatoes, diced

6 cloves garlic, finely chopped

1 gallon fish stock (page 117)

1¹/₂ pounds tuna, cut into 2-inch pieces

5 sprigs parsley, coarsely chopped

1 bunch cilantro, leaves coarsely chopped

Salt and freshly ground black pepper

1 red onion, thinly sliced

6 limes, quartered

Corn nuts

1. Place the yuca in a large stockpot and add water to cover. Bring to a boil, then decrease the heat and simmer gently for about 30 minutes. Remove from the heat and let cool in the water.

2. Heat the oil in a separate stockpot over high heat. Add the onion and half of the tomatoes and cook for 10 minutes. Add the garlic and stock, and bring to a boil. Decrease the heat to low and simmer for 20 minutes. Add the tuna and yuca and cook for 5 minutes.

3. Stir in the parsley and cilantro and season to taste with salt and pepper. Immediately ladle the soup into bowls. Float some of the red onion slices on the surface of each soup, and top with the remaining diced tomatoes. Squeeze lime juice over the onions and sprinkle the corn nuts over the onions and tomatoes. Serve with the remaining lime wedges on the side.

guiso de maíz con cangrejo
[corn stew with crab]

This recipe also appears in *Nuevo Latino*, where I wrote that one of my earliest cooking memories was watching my grandmother make this dish. I actually learned the recipe just by watching her make it so many times. I would only eat it when my grandmother made it, and never when my mother made it, because she didn't use the lard, and it never tasted as good. I'm not fond of using lard, but when it contributes an essential flavor to a classic dish, I'm not willing to compromise.

SERVES 4

$^1/_2$ cup lard

1 white onion, diced (about 1 cup)

$^1/_2$ red bell pepper, diced (about $^1/_2$ cup)

$^1/_2$ green bell pepper, diced (about $^1/_2$ cup)

1 tablespoon finely minced garlic

6 to 8 ears sweet corn, shucked and kernels cut off cobs (about 4 cups)

1 pound yellow fingerling potatoes, peeled and cut into $^1/_2$-inch pieces

1 quart water

1 quart lobster stock (page 117)

3 tablespoons tomato paste

Salt and freshly ground black pepper

1 pound lump crabmeat

1. Melt the lard in a large skillet over medium-high heat. Add the onion, bell peppers, and garlic and sauté for 20 minutes, stirring frequently.

2. Add the corn kernels and cook for another 10 minutes, stirring occasionally. Add the potatoes, water, and stock. Whisk in the tomato paste. Season to taste with salt and pepper. Decrease the heat and simmer for 1 hour, or until the potatoes are tender. Add the crabmeat and simmer for 10 more minutes.

3. Ladle the soup into bowls and serve.

fanesca
[29-ingredient Lent soup]

This Ecuadorean soup is usually made during Lent, when observant Catholics are prohibited from eating meat. The weekend before Lent, each household makes an extremely big batch and eats it throughout the following week. There's no way to make a small batch because there are so many ingredients, but I scaled down the recipe to use 1 cup of each ingredient instead of the usual 4-cup proportions. The main ingredient is the bacalao (salt-cured cod), and there's no substitute for its fermented fish flavor. I tried making the soup with fresh cod, but it didn't have the same character.

Serves 6 to 8

1 pound boneless, skinless bacalao

1 cup dried Lima beans

1 cup brown lentils

1 cup dried great Northern
    white beans

1 cup 1-inch chunks calabaza flesh

2 teaspoons olive oil

1/2 cup 1-inch chunks zucchini

2 white onions, diced

1 red bell pepper, diced

1 green bell pepper, diced

2 tomatoes, diced

1 cup snapped green beans

4 cloves garlic, minced

1 tablespoon peeled and grated
    fresh ginger

1 carrot, peeled and diced

1 stalk celery, diced

1 teaspoon dried oregano

1 teaspoon ground cumin

2 bay leaves

1 quart heavy cream

1 tablespoon crushed red pepper
    flakes

1 cup sweet corn kernels

1 cup cooked long-grain white rice
    (page 114)

1 cup shredded green cabbage

1 cup sweet peas, frozen

1/2 cup ground unsalted toasted
    peanuts

1/2 cup smooth peanut butter

Salt and freshly ground black pepper

1 cup queso fresco

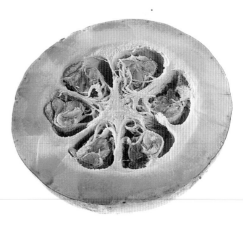

1. Soak the bacalao in water to cover for about 12 hours. Drain and discard the water. Place the fish in a 10-quart stockpot and add water to cover. Simmer 1 hour.

2. While the fish is simmering, prepare the legumes and vegetables: Place the Lima beans in a saucepan and add water to cover. Cook over medium-high heat for 40 minutes, then drain. Place the lentils in a saucepan and add water to cover. Cook over medium-high heat for 20 minutes, then drain. Place the white beans in a saucepan and add water to cover. Cook over medium-high heat for 15 minutes, then drain. Place the calabaza in a small saucepan and add water to cover. Cook over medium-high heat for 10 minutes, then drain. Heat 1 teaspoon of the oil in a small sauté pan over medium heat. Add the zucchini, onions, bell peppers, and tomatoes, and sauté for 3 minutes. Place the green beans in a small saucepan and add water to cover. Cook over medium-high heat for 3 minutes, then drain.

3. When the fish has finished simmering, remove it from the stockpot and set aside to cool. Pour the simmering water into a large liquid measure and reserve.

4. Heat the remaining teaspoon of oil in the stockpot over high heat. Add the onions, bell peppers, tomatoes, garlic, ginger, carrot, and celery. Stir and cook for 10 minutes. Stir in the oregano, cumin, and bay leaves. Add the reserved water and let the mixture come to a boil. Decrease the heat to low and simmer.

5. Using two forks, shred the bacalao. Add the fish and cream to the stockpot. Add the precooked legumes and vegetables, the pepper flakes, corn, rice, cabbage, peas, peanuts, and peanut butter. Season to taste with salt and pepper. Cook for 15 minutes.

6. Ladle the soup into deep bowls. Sprinkle some of the cheese over each bowl and serve.

biche manabita
[snapper stew]

This soup comes from Manabi, a province of Ecuador, where it may have originally been made with a type of trout found there. I've substituted snapper for the trout because rich trout can overwhelm the vegetables. Combining peanuts or peanut butter and green plantains is common in Ecuador. Used together in the dumplings, they give this soup an extra earthy, nutty flavor.

SERVES 6 TO 8

2 green plantains, peeled and finely grated

1 tablespoon peanut butter

1 tablespoon achiote oil (page 115)

1 tablespoon salt

1 teaspoon freshly ground black pepper

————

1/4 cup achiote oil

1 red onion, diced

1 white onion, diced

2 red bell peppers, diced

8 cloves garlic

7 jalapeño chiles

1 gallon fish stock (page 117)

3/4 cup smooth peanut butter

1 ear sweet corn, cut crosswise into 1/2-inch-thick pinwheels

1 ripe plantain, including black skin, cut crosswise into 1/2-inch-thick slices

1 sweet potato, diced

1 yuca, peeled, cored, and diced (about 1 cup)

6 ounces calabaza flesh, diced (about 1 cup)

1 pound snapper fillet, diced

3 sprigs cilantro

Cucumber wedges

2 to 4 limes, quartered

1. In a mixing bowl, combine the green plantains, peanut butter, achiote oil, and salt and pepper. Using your hands, shape into 1/2-inch balls and set aside on a tray lined with waxed paper.

2. Heat the achiote oil in a large stockpot over high heat. Add the onions, bell peppers, garlic, and jalapeños and sauté for 3 to 4 minutes. Add the stock and bring to a boil. Stir in the peanut butter. Add the corn, ripe plantain, sweet potato, yuca, and calabaza. Decrease the heat to low and simmer for 35 to 40 minutes.

3. Add the plantain balls to the soup and cook for 10 minutes.

4. Add the fish and cook another 10 minutes.

5. Coarsely chop the cilantro. Ladle the soup into bowls. Sprinkle some of the cilantro over each bowl. Lightly salt the cucumber slices, then float some on the surface of the soup. Serve with the lime wedges on the side. Squeeze lime juice over the soup before eating.

HARiNa CON CaNGReJO
[CORN MuSH WiTH CRaB]

My Aunt Teresa used to make this all the
time. She used whole blue point crabs but
I use crabmeat instead, because you don't
have to work so hard to enjoy your meal.
Serve the porridge and stew in separate
bowls; as you spoon up the spicy, tomatoey stew, periodically eat a spoonful of
the mild porridge to give your taste buds
a break from the heat and texture of the
stew. With a salad, this is also a dinner in
itself. *(Pictured on back cover, top left.)*

SERVES 4

6 tablespoons olive oil
1 large white onion, diced
   (about 1 cup)
1 large red bell pepper, diced
   (about 1 cup)
1/2 cup diced roasted red bell pepper
   (page 121)
2 plum tomatoes, seeded and diced
10 cachucha chiles, stemmed, seeded,
   and finely diced
4 jalapeno chiles, stemmed and diced
   (including seeds)
2 bay leaves
3 cloves garlic
1 tablespoon red wine vinegar
1/2 cup dry sherry
Salt
Freshly ground black pepper

1 teaspoon crushed red pepper flakes
2 pounds lump jumbo crabmeat
1 cup cream of corn
4 cups water
2 tablespoons sugar
1/4 cup grated manchego cheese
1 cup fine cornmeal

1. Heat the oil in a sauté pan over high
   heat. Add the onion and sauté 2 minutes,
   then add the bell pepper, tomatoes,
   cachuchas, jalapeños, bay leaves, and garlic and sauté another 2 minutes.

2. Pour the vinegar and sherry into the pan
   and deglaze, scraping up any bits clinging
   to the bottom of the pan. Decrease the
   heat to low, cover, and simmer until the
   tomatoes cook down and bind the stew,
   about 10 minutes. Add the pepper flakes
   and season to taste with salt and pepper.

3. Meanwhile, purée the cream of corn,
   water, and sugar in a blender. Transfer the
   puréed mixture to a saucepan and bring
   to a boil over medium-high heat. Stir in
   the cheese. Whisk in the remaining
   2 tablespoons of oil. Whisk in the cornmeal. Season with the salt and pepper.

4. Spoon the porridge and stew into separate bowls and serve immediately.

chipi chipi
[venezuelan clam soup]

Chipi chipis are delicious tiny Venezuelan clams that no doubt inspired this traditional soup. Not unlike the more common Manila clams, which I like to substitute for them, *chipi chipis* have more wide ridges than the manilas have on their shells, and they are smaller and brinier tasting. I added a little ginger to give the soup some zing. Don't forget to add that lime (or lemon) juice at the end.

SERVES 4 TO 6

2 quarts bottled clam juice
1 quart water
1 cup potatoes, peeled and diced
1 cup carrots, peeled and diced
1 cup celery, diced
6 tablespoons butter, softened
1 red onion, diced
1 teaspoon peeled, grated ginger
8 cloves garlic, pounded into a paste
3 pounds chipi chipi or Manila clams,
*   open shells discarded*
4 cups dry white wine
Salt and freshly ground black pepper
2 tablespoons minced cilantro leaves
2 tablespoons flat-leaf parsley leaves
1 lime, quartered

1. In a large stockpot, bring the clam juice and water to a boil. Add the potatoes, carrots, and celery, and cook 15 minutes. Remove from the heat.

2. In a saucepan over high heat, melt 3 tablespoons of the butter. Add half of the onion, garlic, ginger, clams, and wine. Cover and steam about 4 minutes. Uncover and shake the pan vigorously, until the clams open, about 3 minutes. Discard any unopened clams, then cover pan and set aside. Using another saucepan, repeat with the remaining onion, garlic, clams, and wine. Season to taste with salt and pepper.

3. Distribute the clams and liquid among the bowls. Sprinkle the cilantro and parsley over the bowls and serve with the lime wedges on the side. Squeeze lime juice over the soup before eating.

fosforito margariteño
[matchmaking soup
from margarita]

Fosforito means match, and this fiery seafood soup could very well spark passion between two Margariteños—the natives of Margarita, a beautiful island off the coast of Venezuela. This South American–style cioppino is a good example of how Margariteños enjoy their wealth of local seafood. The first time I had this soup was at a restaurant right on the water in Margarita. They put shrimp, calamari, and snapper in their soup, so I based my recipe on theirs. Since then, I've eaten it various places where it was made with scallops or other seafood; it's never the same in any two places. In Margarita, they served it with saffron rice, peas, *arepas* (white corn cakes), and *crema nata,* which is uncultured sour cream, or crème fraîche. Without or without these sides, the soup is a full meal.

SERVES *4* TO *6*

    3 tablespoons achiote oil (page 115)
    1 white onion, diced
    6 cloves garlic, chopped
    8 jalapeño chiles, stemmed and diced
       (including seeds)
    2 small carrots, peeled and diced
    4 stalks celery, diced
    1 bottle (750 ml) dry white wine

2 tablespoons tomato paste
2 quarts shrimp stock (page 119)
2 quarts fish stock (page 117)
1 pound medium shrimp
1 pound red snapper, sliced
*1 pound squid, cleaned and cut
   into rings*
5 plum tomatoes, diced
5 sprigs parsley
5 sprigs cilantro
Salt and freshly ground black pepper
1 lime, quartered

1. Heat the achiote oil in a large stockpot over high heat. Add the onion, garlic, jalapeños, carrots, and celery and cook about 7 minutes. Add the wine and cook 3 minutes. Add the tomato paste and shrimp and fish stocks. Bring the mixture to a boil. Decrease the heat, cover, and simmer for 15 minutes.

2. Uncover the stockpot and add the shrimp, snapper, squid, and tomatoes and stir. Stir in the parsley and cilantro, and season to taste with salt and pepper. Cover, turn off the heat, and let rest for about 5 minutes.

3. Ladle the soup into bowls and serve with the lime wedges on the side. Squeeze the lime juice over the soup before eating.

CHOROS
[mussel soup]

Choro means "mussels" in Peru, which is where I got the inspiration for the recipe. It's thickened with a little bit of bread and is slightly spicy. The cucumber adds crunch and freshness, but the red onions are what make the flavors pop. This soup is good with a glass of dry white wine.

SERVES *4*

> $^1/_4$ *cup olive oil*
>
> *6 cloves garlic, crushed*
>
> *4 pounds mussels, open shells discarded*
>
> *1 bottle (750 ml) dry white wine*
>
> *1 pint heavy cream*
>
> *Zest of 3 lemons*
>
> *3 panca chiles, stemmed and seeded*
>
> *2 ají amarillo peppers, stemmed and seeded*
>
> *2 cups Pisco*
>
> *2 quarts fish stock (page 117)*
>
> *10 plum tomatoes, finely diced*
>
> *3 red bell peppers, finely diced*
>
> *2 cucumbers, peeled, seedy cores removed, and diced*
>
> *3 tablespoons tomato paste*
>
> *1 pound red snapper fillets*
>
> *1 cup diced dried Italian or French bread*
>
> *8 sprigs flat-leaf parsley*
>
> *6 sprigs cilantro*
>
> $^1/_2$ *red onion, thinly sliced*

1. In an 18-inch or larger sauté pan with high sides, heat 1 tablespoon of the oil over high heat. Add one-fourth of the garlic and 1 pound of the mussels. Immediately add a scant $^3/_4$ cup of the wine and $^1/_2$ cup of the cream and cover. Cook about 3 minutes, shaking the pan vigorously. Uncover the pan, sprinkle one-fourth of the zest over the mussels and cook 3 more minutes, or until the mussels have opened. Transfer the mussels and liquid to a large stockpot. Repeat three times. Discard any unopened mussels.

2. In a small mixing bowl, soak the chiles in the Pisco for 1 hour. Transfer the chiles and Pisco to a blender and purée.

3. In an 8-quart stockpot over high heat, combine the stock, tomatoes, bell peppers, cucumbers, tomato paste, red snapper, and Pisco-chile purée. Bring to a boil, then add the diced bread cubes. Decrease the heat to low, cover, and simmer for 35 minutes. Add the mussels. Coarsely chop the parsley and cilantro leaves, then stir into the soup.

4. Ladle the soup into large bowls. Float some of the red onion rings on the surface of the soup and serve.

chupe de marisco
[Lick-your-fingers-good seafood chowder]

Chupes are South American chowders, usually made with potatoes, vegetables, and some type of meat or seafood for flavoring. *Chupe* might have derived from the Spanish word *chupar*, which means "to suck" or "to absorb." Chupes are so delicious, you'll want to run your finger around the inside of the bowl and lick off every last drop. South Americans believe that a chupe is no good if it doesn't make you sweat. So the soup has to be spicy and served piping hot. I like to use big shrimp because I think it's important to see their color and half-moon shape in the soup. A classical garnish for this soup would be hard-boiled eggs, but it's delicious with or without them. With a salad and a piece of country-style bread, this soup is a meal.

SERVES 6 TO 8

4 *aji amarillo peppers, stemmed and seeded*

$^1/_2$ *cup Pisco (page 123)*

3 tablespoons achiote oil (page 115)

1 white onion, diced

6 cloves garlic, pounded into a paste

2 red bell peppers, diced

1 teaspoon turmeric

1 teaspoon saffron threads

1 teaspoon crushed red pepper flakes

2 quarts fish stock (page 117)

2 small carrots, peeled and diced

3 stalks celery, diced

4 plum tomatoes, diced

1 teaspoon ground cumin

1 teaspoon dried coriander

3 tablespoons long-grain white rice

3 potatoes, peeled and diced

1 pound medium shrimp

1 pound scallops

1 pound squid, cleaned, body and tentacles sliced

1 cup fresh or frozen peas

3 hard-boiled eggs, chopped

2 limes, quartered

1. Soak the chiles in the Pisco for 30 minutes.

2. Heat the achiote oil in a large stockpot over high heat. Add the onion, garlic, and bell peppers and sauté for 3 minutes, stirring often. Add the turmeric, saffron, and pepper flakes. Add the Pisco and chiles and let the alcohol cook out, about 5 minutes. Add the stock, carrots, celery, tomatoes, cumin, and coriander, and bring to a boil. Decrease the heat to low, add the rice, and simmer for 15 minutes. Add the potatoes and simmer for 10 more minutes. Turn off the heat, add the seafood, cover, and let rest for 10 minutes.

3. Add the peas, then ladle the soup into bowls. Sprinkle some egg over each of the bowls and serve with the lime wedges on the side.

chupe de camarones

[Lick-your-fingers-good shrimp chowder]

I've eaten many different versions of this soup; this recipe is my take on the basic formula. Turmeric, which makes the soup bright yellow, is one of the key ingredients, as is the *huacatay*, a black mint from Peru. Mint is probably the best substitute, but it's a little stronger and doesn't have the slight cilantro flavor of *huacatay*. Served with white rice on the side (see page 114), this soup becomes a full meal. A few generous squeezes of lime juice is mandatory to finish it, and so is a dash or two of the hot sauce of your choice. I leave the heads on the shrimp, but you may remove them if you like. The fatty, pastelike substance in the head of the shrimp gives the soup an incredibly shrimpy flavor.

SERVES 4

- *3 tablespoons achiote oil (page 115)*
- *1 white onion, diced*
- *6 cloves garlic, diced*
- *1 red bell pepper, diced*
- *6 jalapeño chiles, stemmed and diced (including seeds)*
- *1 teaspoon turmeric*
- *1 tablespoon saffron threads*
- *1 teaspoon Colman's mustard powder*
- *1 cup dry white wine*
- *1 gallon shrimp stock (page 119)*
- *2 carrots, peeled and diced*
- *3 stalks celery, diced*
- *3 new potatoes, diced*
- *2 tablespoons diced ají amarillo chile*
- *3 plum tomatoes, diced*
- *8 sprigs huacatay, mint, or cilantro*
- *1 pound medium shrimp, heads on, peeled and deveined*
- *Salt and freshly ground black pepper*

1. Heat the oil in a large stockpot over high heat. Add the onion, garlic, bell pepper, and jalapeños and stir. Cook about 3 minutes, then add the turmeric, saffron, and mustard powder. Cook another 3 minutes.

2. Add the wine and cook 2 more minutes, or until all the alcohol evaporates, then add the stock, carrots, celery, and potatoes. Bring the mixture to a boil and let boil for 5 minutes. Decrease the heat to low, add the ají chile and tomatoes, and simmer for 20 minutes.

3. Coarsely chop the cilantro leaves. Add the shrimp and cilantro to the soup and season to taste with salt and pepper. Cook 5 to 7 minutes.

4. Ladle the soup into bowls and serve immediately.

vatapá
[thick and coconuty snapper and shrimp soup]

The classical recipe for this makes a really thick stewlike soup, almost like a polenta. I make mine more brothy and souplike, yet still thick. The coconut milk, dried shrimp, peanuts, and cashews give it an African flair. Serve it with white rice (see page 114) and some pickled hot peppers on the side. It's an excellent main course.

Serves 4

7 ounces stale French bread, cubed

1 5-ounce can evaporated milk

2 quarts fish stock (page 117)

4 green onions, white parts only, thinly sliced

1 ounce fresh ginger, peeled and grated

2 cloves garlic

8 ounces red snapper fillet, skin removed, diced

8 ounces rock shrimp, peeled

$1/_2$ cup ground dried shrimp

$1/_2$ cup ground toasted, unsalted peanuts

$1/_2$ cup ground toasted, unsalted cashews

1 14-ounce can coconut milk

$1/_2$ teaspoon ground mace

2 tablespoons dendê oil

Salt and freshly ground black pepper

2 cups cooked white rice (page 114)

1. Soak bread cubes in evaporated milk to moisten, about 5 minutes. Using your hands, squeeze excess milk out of bread and reserve.

2. In a stockpot over medium-high heat, bring the stock, green onions, ginger, and garlic to a boil. Decrease the heat to low, add the fish, cover, and simmer for 10 minutes. Strain, reserving the fish stock.

3. Place the fish and other strained ingredients in the bowl of a food processor. Add the rock shrimp and bread. Process until completely puréed.

4. In a clean stockpot, bring the strained stock to a boil. Whisk in the dried shrimp and nuts. Cook about 10 minutes, then whisk in the puréed fish mixture. Decrease the heat to low, then add the coconut milk, mace, and dendê oil. Cover and simmer for 20 more minutes. Season to taste with salt and pepper.

5. Spoon some of the rice into each serving bowl. Ladle the soup over the rice and serve.

sopa erizo de mar
[sea urchin soup]

On a trip to the town of Viña del Mar in Chile, I went to a restaurant called *Los Marineros,* or "the sailors," and it was right on the waterfront. The owners had a boat and caught their own fish. That night, I tried a lot of seafood I had never tried before. One of the most memorable items they made for me was sea urchin puréed with lime juice, garlic, and cream served in a shot glass like a shooter. They swore it was an aphrodisiac. That's where I got the idea to make this hot sea urchin soup and serve it in the shell. It's a hit at Patria. Sea urchin has a nice buttery, briny flavor that is totally amazing, but it's very high in cholesterol. When the meat is removed from the shell, it looks like small tongues. Look for it in Japanese markets.

SERVES 4

2 tablespoons sweet butter
1 small white onion, diced
2 cloves garlic, crushed
3 teaspoons soy sauce
1 sweet potato, peeled and diced
1 small carrot, peeled and grated
2 cups dry white wine
3 quarts bottled clam juice
1 cup heavy cream
1 pound sea urchin
Black sesame seeds
3 limes, quartered

1. In a stockpot over medium heat, melt the butter. Add the onion and garlic and sauté. Add the soy sauce and cook 3 minutes. Add the sweet potato and carrot. Add the wine and reduce for 5 minutes. Add the clam juice and cream, decrease the heat to low, and simmer for 45 minutes.

2. Add the sea urchin while puréeing the soup with a handheld blender.

3. Ladle the soup into bowls. Sprinkle some of the sesame seeds over the soup and serve with lime wedges on the side. Squeeze lime juice over the soup before eating.

moqueca
[tomato—coconut milk soup with swordfish and shrimp]

Moqueca is another classical dish from coastal Brazil. This particular recipe was developed by a good friend who cooked it for my wife and I one day, and it was unbelievably good. It's a tomatoey, coconuty broth with a little spice. He serves it with toasted yuca flour, called *farofa*, mixed with butter and garlic, to be periodically sprinkled over the soup as it's eaten. Moqueca is especially good with a *caipirinha*, a Brazilian drink made with fresh limes, a bit of sugar, and a sugarcane liquor called *cachaça*.

SERVES 4

3 tablespoons dendê oil
1 red bell pepper, diced
1 yellow bell pepper, diced
10 cachucha chiles, stemmed, seeded, and chopped
1 habanero chile, stemmed, seeded, and chopped
1 white onion, thinly sliced
6 plum tomatoes, seeded and diced (page 121)
3 tablespoons tomato paste
1 quart fish stock (page 117)
6 sprigs thyme, leaves removed and stems discarded
6 sprigs cilantro, leaves coarsely chopped
1 14-ounce can coconut milk
1 pound swordfish loin, cut into 4 equal slices
1 pound medium shrimp, peeled and deveined
1/2 cup toasted unsalted cashews, chopped
2 cups cooked white rice (page 114)

1. Heat the dendê oil in a stockpot over medium heat. Add the bell peppers, chiles, and onion and sauté about 10 minutes. Add the tomatoes, tomato paste, stock, thyme, and half of the cilantro. Increase the heat to high and bring to a boil. Decrease the heat to low, add the coconut milk, and let the soup slow to a simmer. Add the swordfish and simmer 10 minutes. Add the shrimp and simmer 3 more minutes. Turn off the heat, add the cashews and stir the remaining cilantro. Cover and let rest 5 minutes.

2. Divide the rice among the bowls. Ladle the soup over the rice and serve.

zarzuela de mariscos
[seafood soup operetta]

This soup is a little more complicated
than most because it has several steps
and requires that you know intuitively
when to add the ingredients to the pot to
keep from over- or undercooking them.
Zarzuela is a Spanish opera, musical
comedy, or operetta, and that's what this
dish is—an operetta of seafood.

SERVES 4

12 cherrystone clams,
    open shells discarded

1 quart milk

$^1\!/_2$ cup flour

$^1\!/_2$ teaspoon salt

1 teaspoon freshly ground
    black pepper

8 ounces snapper fillet with skin on,
    cut into 6 small pieces

3 tablespoons olive oil

1 onion, coarsely diced (about 1 cup)

2 teaspoons pulverized garlic
    (with mortar and pestle)

4 plum tomatoes, coarsely diced

1 red bell pepper, diced (about 1 cup)

1 tablespoon Spanish paprika

1 ounce fresh ginger, peeled and diced

1 teaspoon ground chipotle
    chile powder

2 cups dry white wine

1 cup almond flour

$^1\!/_2$ gallon lobster stock (page 117)

3 lobster tails, split

1 pound large shrimp, peeled and
    deveined, shells reserved

$^1\!/_2$ pound squid, cleaned, body cut
    into rings, tentacles cut into pieces

1. Scrub the clam shells, then place the
   clams in a bowl and cover with the milk.
   Soak in the refrigerator overnight.

2. The next day, combine the flour, salt, and
   pepper in a mixing bowl. Dredge the
   snapper in the flour mixture.

3. Heat the oil in a heavy-bottomed stockpot over high heat. Add the snapper to
   the pan, cook on only one side until
   opaque and slightly flaky, then remove
   and set aside. Drain the clams, again discarding any open shells.

4. Add the onion, garlic, tomatoes, bell pepper, paprika, ginger, chipotle, and clams to
   the stockpot and cook about 5 minutes, or
   until the clams open. Add the wine and
   cook 4 more minutes. Stir in the almond
   flour. Add the stock and bring to a boil.
   Add the lobster and cook 2 minutes. Add
   the shrimp and cook 2 minutes. Add the
   snapper and cook 2 minutes. Add the
   squid and cook 3 more minutes.

5. Ladle the soup into bowls, discard any
   unopened clams, and serve.

puré de chícharos

sopa de frijoles colorados

tamal en cazuela

sopa de frijoles negros

sopa de frijoles media Luna

caldo gallego

caldo de elote

sopa de maíz y maní

sopa de quinoa

pozole blanco

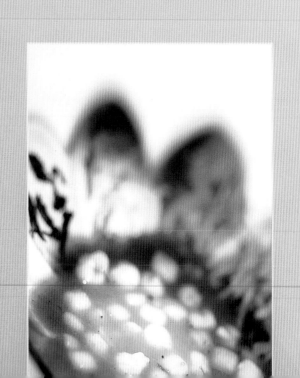

bean- and grain-based soups

porotos con riendas

sopa de frisoles

sopa de lentejas negras
y calamares

maíz con chorizo

asopado de gandules
con arroz

sopa de huitlacoche

sopa de garbanzos
y camarones secos

sopa de habas

puré de chícharos
[simple split pea soup]

I've tried making this soup vegetarian, but it's just not the same because the smokiness of the ham stock and bacon really complement the sweetness of the split peas. I like to add a palmful of fresh thyme—it makes the flavors of the pork and peas work together even better.

SERVES 4 TO 6

> *6 ounces bacon, diced*
>
> *1 small yellow onion, diced*
>
> *4 to 6 carrots, peeled and diced (about 2 cups)*
>
> *2 large potatoes, peeled and diced (about 2 cups)*
>
> *3 bay leaves*
>
> *4 cloves garlic, chopped*
>
> *4 quarts ham stock (page 118)*
>
> *14 ounces dried split green peas*
>
> *Salt and freshly ground black pepper*
>
> *6 sprigs thyme*

1. Heat a heavy-bottomed stockpot over medium heat. Add the bacon and cook about 5 minutes, stirring continuously.

2. Add the onion, carrots, potatoes, and bay leaves to the stockpot and sauté about 5 minutes.

3. Add the garlic to the stockpot and raise the heat to high. Sauté 2 more minutes. Add the ham stock and split peas. Bring to a boil, then decrease heat to low, cover, and simmer for 1 hour.

4. Stir and season with salt and pepper. Mince the thyme and stir into the soup. Purée the soup with a handheld blender. Ladle into bowls and serve.

sopa de
frijoles colorados
[red bean soup]

All I have to do is see this soup, and it reminds me of my father. Every dinner, for as long as I can remember, my father has had rice and beans. He always has the same type of rice—basic long-grain white—with different beans, but red beans are his favorite. This is my father's recipe, which he has perfected the old-fashioned way: by making it again and again and again. Adding the plantain is optional; a lot of the time, I don't put it in. This soup, or pottage, I should say, is a meal in itself.

SERVES 4

3 tablespoons olive oil
6 ounces bacon
1 large white onion, diced
8 ounces ham, diced
4 bay leaves
3 cloves garlic
1 red bell pepper, diced
1 green bell pepper, diced
*14 ounces red beans, soaked
  overnight and drained*
1 cup diced chorizo
2 potatoes, peeled and diced
1 semiripe plantain, peeled and diced

1 cup diced calabaza flesh
1 teaspoon ground cumin
Salt and freshly ground black pepper
*2 cups cooked long-grain white rice
  (page 114)*

1. Heat a heavy-bottomed stockpot over medium heat, add the oil and bacon, and render about 5 minutes. Add the onion and ham and cook 3 more minutes. Add the bay leaves. Cook 2 minutes.

2. Add the garlic, peppers, and the beans with the water they were soaking in. Raise the heat to high and bring to a boil. Cook for 10 minutes.

3. Decrease the heat, cover and simmer for 1 hour.

4. Add the chorizo, potatoes, and plantain and cook 30 minutes. Add the calabaza and cook 20 more minutes. Add the cumin, salt, and pepper and adjust the seasonings to taste.

5. Place the rice in four bowls. Ladle the soup over the rice and serve.

tamaL eN cazueLa
[tamaLes iN a pot]

In Cuba, as in other Latin American countries, most home cooks only make tamales a few times a year—usually during the holidays, and mainly for Christmas and Lent—because they are so time-consuming. These days, as people get busier and busier, many are skipping the tamale making and just cooking up this thick polentalike soup. I like to serve my version with grilled fish. It's a really good combination—the smokiness from the grill and natural sweetness of the corn are perfect partners.

SERVES 4

8 ears corn, kernels cut off the cobs
1 cup sofrito (page 115)
2 cups water
2 tablespoons sugar
6 ounces lard
1 pound pork loin, diced
1 small white onion, finely diced
2 cloves garlic, minced
1 red bell pepper, diced
1 green bell pepper, diced
Salt

1. In a blender, purée the corn, sofrito, 1 cup of the water, and the sugar on high speed in batches.

2. In a heavy-bottomed stockpot, melt the lard over medium heat. Add the pork and cook for 7 to 10 minutes, or until no trace of pink remains in the meat. Add the onion, garlic, and bell peppers and cook 5 more minutes. Add the puréed corn mixture and the remaining cup of water. Decrease the heat and simmer, periodically skimming off any impurities that rise to the surface of the soup.

3. Simmer the soup for 30 more minutes, or until thick. Season with salt and serve in bowls.

sopa de frijoles negros
[black bean soup]

This is a special black bean soup because it's puréed and uses a roasted chicken stock, which adds a smokiness that enhances the mellowness of the beans. The first time I had a soup like this was at Gabriel's in Washington, D.C. When I asked the chef about the recipe, he credited an employee from Guatemala. I always eat this soup with a generous dollop of sour cream and a scoop of fresh tomato salsa on top.

SERVES 4 TO 6

1 white onion, peeled
1 red bell pepper
4 jalapeño chiles
1 gallon roasted chicken stock
(page 118)
1 pound black beans
10 cloves garlic
3 bay leaves
1 tablespoon dried oregano
1 teaspoon ground cumin
1 tablespoon dried ancho chile powder
1 teaspoon dried chipotle chile powder
4 ounces lard
Salt
*6 sprigs cilantro, leaves removed
    and stems discarded
    (about 2 tablespoons)*
Sour cream
Salsa

1. Spear the onion with a fork and roast over a high flame, holding it approximately 4 inches above the heat and turning continuously until evenly charred and aromatic. Set aside to cool. Repeat with the bell pepper and jalapeños. Alternatively, cut the onion in half and roast with the whole peppers on a baking sheet under the broiler, turning the peppers regularly so they blacken evenly. When cool, remove the seeds and stem from the bell pepper and the stems from the jalapeños. (Leave on the charred skin.)

2. In a large stockpot, combine the stock, beans, 5 cloves of garlic, bay leaves, oregano, cumin, and chile powders. Over low heat, bring to a slow, rolling simmer. Let simmer, covered, for 30 minutes to 1 hour. Add charred vegetables and simmer 30 more minutes.

3. In a sauté pan over medium heat, melt the lard. Add the remaining 5 cloves of garlic and sauté, stirring often, until golden brown. Add to the stockpot and season with salt to taste. Add the cilantro. Purée the soup with a handheld blender until smooth.

4. Ladle into bowls, garnish with a spoonful of sour cream and salsa, and serve.

sopa de frijoles media Luna
[Lima bean soup]

Limas are one of my favorite beans. They are also one of the primary cash crops of Colombia. Limas have a buttery richness that no other bean can match. This is a foolproof soup, so easy to make and loaded with flavor—it's one of my favorites. Named for the capital of Peru, Lima beans may have been one of the first crops cultivated by South America's indigenous farmers. Some varieties are said to grow as large in diameter as a doorknob. We've tested this recipe several times using different varieties, but I'm most fond of giant Peruvian Lima beans, which are about the size of a quarter. Their flavor is even more buttery and "beany" than the common varieties.

SERVES 4 TO 6

2 ounces lard

4 ounces salt pork, diced

1 large white onion, diced

8 ounces smoked ham, diced

1 gallon water

1 pound dried Lima beans, soaked 2 hours and drained

4 russet potatoes, peeled and diced

1 bunch collard greens, rinsed and cut into strips

1 pound chorizo, thinly sliced

1. Heat the lard and salt pork in a large stockpot over high heat. Add the onion and diced ham and sauté 6 to 8 minutes, stirring often.

2. Add the water and Lima beans to the stockpot, decrease the heat to medium and cover. Gradually bring the mixture to a slow, rolling boil. When boiling, remove the lid and boil uncovered about 1 hour. Add the potatoes, collards, and chorizo. Cook 20 more minutes.

3. Ladle the soup into bowls and serve.

caldo gallego
[galician white bean soup]

This is one of my favorite soups or one-pot meals—I could eat it all the time. The recipe originally came from Galicia in northern Spain. The humble turnip is actually the element that makes it so wonderful because it gives the soup a nice peppery flavor and cuts the beans' richness. There's a restaurant in Miami, Latin American Cafeteria, that makes a good version. Whenever I'm in town, I have to go there and have a bowl…or two.

SERVES 6

> 8 ounces salt pork, cleaned, trimmed, and cut into 1-inch cubes
>
> 1 large onion, diced
>
> 1 teaspoon mashed garlic (with a mortar and pestle)
>
> 2 ham hocks
>
> 14 ounces dried white or navy beans
>
> 3 bay leaves
>
> 1 gallon ham stock (page 118)
>
> 1 large plus 1 small russet potato, peeled and cubed
>
> 1 pound chorizo
>
> 5 ounces Virginia ham
>
> 1 large turnip, cubed (about 1 cup)
>
> 1 large bunch collard or mustard greens, coarsely chopped (about 1 1/2 loosely packed cups)

1. In a large heavy-bottomed stockpot over low heat, render the salt pork, then add the onion and garlic and cook, but do not brown, for 10 minutes.

2. Add the ham hocks, beans, bay leaves, and stock to the stockpot, increase the heat to high and bring to a boil. When boiling, decrease the heat to low, cover, and simmer for about 45 minutes. Uncover, add the potatoes, chorizo, ham, and turnip and cook for 20 minutes or more.

3. Just before serving, stir in the greens. Ladle the soup into bowls and serve.

caldo de elote
[CORN SOUP]

The secret to this soup is the corn stock. Like the the American Indians who were the first to cook with corn, I wanted to find a use for the cobs, so I tried making a stock with them. They gave the stock so much corn flavor, it earned its name. Don't make this soup unless you make the corn stock to go in it—it won't taste the same without it.

SERVES 4 TO 6

- *2 tablespoons butter*
- *1 white onion, diced*
- *8 ounces shallots*
- *1 tablespoon saffron threads*
- *3 ounces fresh ginger, peeled and sliced*
- *2 dried ají amarillo peppers, stemmed and seeded*
- *1 gallon corn stock (page 116)*
- *12 ears sweet corn*
- *1 tablespoon sugar*
- *chives, cut into 2-inch lengths*

1. In a large stockpot, melt the butter over medium heat. Add the onion, shallots, and saffron, decrease the heat to low, and sweat, about 5 minutes.

2. Add the ginger, chiles, and all but 1 cup of the stock. Bring to a boil, decrease the heat to low, cover, and simmer for 35 minutes.

3. Meanwhile, shuck the corn and cut the kernels off the cobs. Place the corn, 1 cup of the stock, and the sugar in a blender and purée.

4. Whisk the puréed corn into the soup and leave uncovered until ready to serve.

5. Ladle the soup into bowls, garnish with chives and serve.

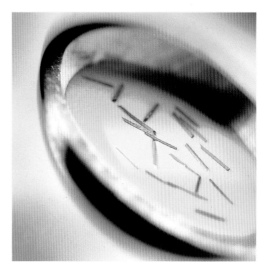

sopa de maíz y maní
[corn and peanut soup]

Some type of peanut soup can be found in most Latin American countries, as peanuts are one of the original crops cultivated by the indigenous people of South and Central America. The hominy in this particular recipe is what really intrigued me. Its nuttiness varies enough from the flavor of the peanuts to give the soup another dimension. I use peanut butter for a nice smooth consistency and dried peanuts to add a little texture. Traditionally, this soup would be made with a beef stock, but I use corn to keep it vegetarian. When you make the corn stock, you'll see that the recipe calls for corn cobs. Many people don't realize how much flavor you can get out of the cobs. After one sip of the corn stock, I promise you'll never want to throw away cobs again.

Serves 4 to 6

1 gallon water

8 ounces hominy

2 tablespoons sweet butter

2 white onions, diced

3 cloves garlic, minced

2 to 4 carrots, peeled and grated (about 2 cups)

2 ounces fresh ginger, peeled and grated

1 gallon corn stock (page 116)

2 cups dry-roasted unsalted peanuts

5 tablespoons smooth peanut butter

4 jalapeño chiles, stemmed and diced (including seeds)

10 ears sweet corn, shucked, kernels cut off cobs and roasted (page 121)

5 sprigs cilantro

1. In a small stockpot over high heat, bring the water and hominy to a boil. Boil for 35 minutes, then drain the hominy and rinse it in cold water.

2. Melt the butter in a large stockpot over high heat. Add the onions, garlic, and carrots and sauté for 10 minutes, stirring often. Add the ginger, stock, peanuts, and peanut butter. Bring to a boil and whisk until the peanut butter is evenly incorporated. Decrease the heat to low, cover, and simmer for 35 minutes.

3. Uncover the stockpot and purée the soup with a handheld blender until smooth. Add the hominy, jalapeños, and roasted corn. Simmer 5 more minutes. Strip the cilantro leaves from the stems and julienne.

4. Ladle the soup into shallow bowls. Sprinkle some of the cilantro leaves over each bowl and serve.

sopa de quinoa
[quinoa soup]

Quinoa is the seed of a leafy annual plant indigenous to the Andes' high-altitude valleys. It is high in protein and similar in taste and texture to cracked wheat. South Americans sometimes eat it in place of rice—it's a staple there, not the gourmet food it is here in the States. Quinoa has an outside coating that can make it taste bitter. Most of the coating is usually removed when the "grain" is processed for consumption, but you should always rinse quinoa under cold running water just to be sure.

SERVES 4

1 gallon chicken stock (page 116)

2 small skinless chicken breast halves

2 bay leaves

3 sprigs thyme

7 cloves garlic, minced

1 tablespoon salt

3 tablespoons sweet butter, softened

1 white onion, diced

1 pound fresh spinach leaves, rinsed, stems removed, and leaves finely chopped

6 sprigs flat-leaf parsley, leaves removed and chopped, stems discarded

1/2 cup loosely packed cilantro leaves

6 sprigs mint, leaves removed and chopped

3 jalapeño chiles, stemmed and diced (including seeds)

1 1/2 cups quinoa

3 stalks celery, diced

5 green onions, white and green parts, finely sliced

1. In a stockpot over high heat, combine the stock, chicken, bay leaves, thyme, 4 of the garlic cloves, and salt. Bring to a boil, then decrease the heat to low, cover, and simmer for 15 minutes.

2. Remove the chicken from the stockpot and set aside to cool.

3. Strain the stock, discarding the bay leaves and thyme.

4. Using two forks, shred the chicken.

5. Heat the butter in a large stockpot over medium heat. Add the onion and the remaining 3 cloves of garlic and sauté for about 5 minutes. Add the spinach, parsley, cilantro, mint, and jalapeños. Cook for about 5 minutes. Add the stock, bring to a boil and cook for about 3 minutes. Decrease the heat to low and add the quinoa, celery, and green onions. Cover and simmer for 35 minutes. Uncover, season to taste with salt, and stir in the chicken.

6. Ladle the soup into deep bowls and serve.

pozoLe bLaNco
[white corn posoLe]

The garnishes give this simple soup its spark. Serve it the way I do: give everyone their own set of little bowls filled with some of each garnish. As they add the garnishes and the amount they like, the soup will assume as many textures and flavors as there are guests at your table. It's definitely a fun soup to serve company.

Serves 6 to 8

> 2 pounds pork butt, fat trimmed
>   and discarded
>
> 1 gallon plus 2 cups water
>
> 3 bay leaves
>
> 1 teaspoon dried oregano
>
> 1 teaspoon ground cumin
>
> 1 tablespoon salt
>
> 10 cloves garlic
>
> 2 tablespoons olive oil
>
> 1 white onion, diced
>
> 8 jalapeño chiles, stemmed and diced
>   (including seeds)
>
> 8 ounces tomatillos, husked and
>   rinsed in warm water
>
> 1 cup tightly packed cilantro leaves
>
> 6 ounces toasted pumpkin seeds
>   (page 121)
>
> 2 cans hominy corn
>
> $^1/_2$ cup diced radish
>
> $^1/_2$ cup diced avocado

> $^1/_2$ cup diced red onion
>
> $^1/_2$ cup sliced green onions, including
>   white and green parts
>
> 2 limes, quartered

1. In a large stockpot over high heat, combine the pork, 1 gallon water, bay leaves, oregano, cumin, salt, and 4 cloves of the garlic. Bring the mixture to a boil, then decrease the heat and simmer for 1 hour. Strain the soup, reserving liquid and returning it to the stockpot. Let the strained meat cool, then shred. Add the remaining 2 cups water to the stockpot.

2. Crush the remaining 6 cloves of garlic. Heat the olive oil in a large sauté pan over medium heat. Add the onion, crushed garlic, jalapeños, and tomatillos, and sauté about 6 minutes. Add the sauté mixture to the stockpot. Add $^1/_2$ cup of the cilantro and the pumpkin seeds. Purée with a handheld blender. Add the pork and hominy. Taste and adjust the seasonings, if necessary.

3. For garnish, place the radishes, remaining cilantro leaves, avocado, and red onion in separate serving bowls. Ladle the soup into bowls and serve with the garnishes.

porotos con riendas
[CRANBERRY BEAN AND pasta soup]

Porotos is the Chilean word for cranberry beans, which are plentiful in Chile. *Riendas* translates to "reins." I guess the spaghetti in the soup reminds Chilean cooks of the reins a horse is guided with. This is one of the soups I enjoyed at the employee cafeteria at the Hyatt in Santiago, Chile, where I learned a lot from the saucier, who made all the soups as well as the sauces. He used fresh cranberry beans, not dried, but fresh ones are so difficult to find in the States during the off-season that I changed the recipe to use dried. This is another simple, delicious soup, the Latin equivalent of Italy's pasta e fajiole.

SERVES 6 TO 8

3 ounces bacon
7 ounces bonelesss smoked ham, diced
1 white onion, finely diced
1 red bell pepper, diced
6 cloves garlic, diced
10 ounces dried cranberry beans
1 gallon chicken stock (page 116)
3 ounces dried spaghetti
1 russet potato, diced
4 plum tomatoes, diced
2 stalks celery, diced
Salt and freshly ground black pepper

1. In a large stockpot over high heat, cook the bacon until it begins to crisp, about 6 minutes. Stir in the ham, onion, bell pepper, and garlic. Stir and cook for 5 more minutes. Add the beans and stock, cover, and bring to a boil. Decrease the heat to low and simmer for 45 minutes.

2. Uncover the stockpot and add the pasta, potato, tomatoes, and celery. Continue to stir and cook for about 10 minutes. Season to taste with salt and pepper. Remove from the heat and let stand, covered, 10 minutes.

3. Ladle the soup into bowls and serve.

sopa de frisoles
[red kidney bean soup]

Free-SO-lays. That's how they say beans in Colombia. Red kidney beans are the frijoles of choice there, where they often serve them with white rice and a fried egg (called *bandeja paisa*). This is an updated version of the many bean recipes cooked throughout Colombia, but it's still a simple bean dish that should be served with rice and a protein source like roasted chicken or pork or pan-fried steak. Don't soak the red kidney beans overnight—if you do, they'll cook too quickly and throw off the preparation times I've given below.

SERVES 4

2 tablespoons olive oil

2 bunches green onions, white and green parts sliced

4 cloves garlic

4 plum tomatoes, diced

1 tablespoon tomato paste

1 gallon water

1 pound red beans

1 pound pork shoulder, cut into small dice

4 ounces salt pork, without skin, diced

2 green plantains, peeled and diced

1 large plus 2 small carrots, grated (about 1 cup)

1 teaspoon ground cumin

Salt and freshly ground black pepper

1. Heat the olive oil in a saucepan over high heat. Add the green onions, garlic, tomatoes, and tomato paste and sauté 3 minutes, stirring occasionally. Let cool, then purée in a blender.

2. In a large stockpot, bring the water, beans, pork shoulder, salt pork, plantains, carrots, and cumin to a boil and continue to boil for 10 minutes. Decrease the heat to low, add the puréed mixture, cover, and simmer 1 hour.

3. Uncover, season to taste with salt and pepper, and let simmer 20 more minutes.

4. Ladle into bowls and serve.

Sopa de Lentejas Negras y Calamares
[Black Lentil and Squid Soup]

This recipe was invented by one of my cooks from Bolivia. He used to make the same Bolivian-style lentil soup all the time, then one day we got in what we called beluga black lentils and decided to try them in his soup. The lentils are beautiful and really black, and make the soup something special. Inspired by the lentils, we also added some calamari and a touch of squid ink to make it even blacker. The soup was an instant hit at Patria. It's very important not to over-cook the squid. You want to throw it in the pot right before you're ready to serve the soup, then immediately take the soup off the fire and just let the squid cook slightly in the hot liquid.

Serves 6 to 8

2 tablespoons achiote oil (page 115)
1 white onion, diced
3 cloves garlic, minced
3 stalks celery, diced
4 plum tomatoes, diced
1 gallon fish stock (page 117)
1 pound black lentils
1 tablespoon squid ink
2 russet potatoes, peeled and diced
2 carrots, peeled and finely diced
1 teaspoon ground cumin
Salt and pepper
8 ounces cleaned squid, including tentacles, finely diced
3 green onions, white and green parts sliced

1. Heat the oil in a large stockpot over high heat. Add the onion, garlic, celery, and tomatoes and sauté for about 10 minutes, stirring often. Add the stock and lentils and bring to a boil. Add the squid ink, potatoes, carrots, and cumin, and continue to boil for 25 minutes.

2. Just before serving, uncover the stockpot, season to taste with salt and pepper, and add the squid and green onions. Turn off the heat, re-cover, and let sit for 10 minutes.

3. Ladle the soup into bowls and serve.

maíz con chorizo
[corn mush with chorizo]

The sharpness of the queso fresco, a traditional Mexican cow's milk cheese similar to feta, and the sweetness of the fresh corn make this home-style porridgelike dish special enough for company or Sunday dinner. Be sure to use very fine or superfine cornmeal; if you use a regular grind, your dish will be gritty.

SERVES 4

2 tablespoons olive oil

1 white onion, julienned

1 red bell pepper, julienned

1 green bell pepper, julienned

1 pound chorizo sausage, cut into 1/2-inch slices

6 cloves garlic, thinly sliced

1 tablespoon ground ancho chile powder

1 tablespoon ground chipotle chile powder

1 14-ounce can tomato sauce

4 ears sweet yellow corn

2 quarts chicken stock (page 116)

2 tablespoons sugar

4 ounces queso fresco or feta cheese

Salt

8 ounces finely ground cornmeal

1. Heat the olive oil in a large sauté pan over high heat. Add the onion and bell peppers and cook 2 minutes. Add the chorizo and continue to cook while stirring. Add the garlic, chile powders, and tomato sauce. Stir and cook 3 more minutes. Keep warm.

2. Shuck the corn, cut the kernels off the cobs, and purée in a blender with 1 cup of the chicken stock and the sugar. Set aside.

3. In a medium stockpot over medium heat, combine the stock, cheese, and corn mixture. Bring to a boil and cook 5 minutes. Season to taste with salt.

4. Add the cornmeal in a slow, steady stream while whisking continuously. Decrease the heat to low or warm, and keep whisking until the soup is barely simmering.

5. Spoon a generous amount of the cornmeal mixture into bowls. Spoon the chorizo mixture over and serve.

asopado de gandules con arroz
[soupy peas and rice]

Asopado means "soupy," and this is just that—a soupy rice dish. It's popular in Puerto Rico, where some make it *asopado,* or wet, style and some make it on the dry side. I like to make it with fresh pigeon peas because they have a much cleaner flavor than the dried, but they can be difficult to find so I've used dried in this recipe. If you were to use fresh pigeon peas, you wouldn't have to presoak or cook them for a whole hour. This is not a main dish, but it's great dish to serve with roasted pork or chicken.

SERVES 4

12 ounces dried pigeon peas, soaked in water overnight

1 gallon water

4 bay leaves

¹/₄ cup achiote oil (page 115)

6 ounces salt pork, skinned and diced

8 ounces cured ham, diced

1 large white onion, diced

2 tablespoons chopped garlic

¹/₂ green bell pepper, diced (about ¹/₂ cup)

¹/₂ red bell pepper, diced (about ¹/₂ cup)

4 ounces cachucha chiles, stemmed, seeded, and diced (about ¹/₃ cup)

1 cup tomato, diced

3 tablespoons tomato paste

5 cups chicken stock (page 116)

1 cup uncooked long-grain white rice

3 to 4 culantro leaves, minced

Salt

Freshly ground black pepper

Salsa

1. Drain the peas, place in a stockpot, and add the water and bay leaves. Bring to a boil over high heat, then decrease the heat to low and simmer for 1 hour or until peas are tender. Drain, rinse, and reserve the peas.

2. Heat the oil in a stockpot over medium heat. Add the salt pork and cook to render fat, about 5 minutes. Remove the pork and set aside.

3. Add the cured ham, onion, garlic, bell peppers, cachucha chiles, and tomato to the stockpot and cook for another 5 minutes. Add the stock and rice and bring to a boil. Decrease the heat to low, stir in the tomato paste, and simmer for 40 minutes.

4. Season the soup to taste, with salt and pepper. Add the pigeon peas and culantro and cook 5 minutes, or just until the peas are heated through.

5. Ladle the soup into bowls and serve with salsa.

sopa de huitlacoche
[corn "truffle" soup]

Huitlacoche is a fungus that grows on corn ears during the rainy season in Mexico and a few U.S. states. It's an acquired taste, very rich and often described as a cornlike truffle. Its flavor is maximized when combined with chiles, lots of cilantro, the Latin American herb epazote, and salt. In this soup, roasting the vegetables and potatoes also enhances the flavor of the huitlacoche. Fresh or frozen huitlacoche is occasionally available in gourmet markets (or to order it through the mail, see page 124), but you'll probably have better luck finding canned huitlacoche from Mexico, which works well enough. There's a very fine line between under- and oversalting and overchile-ing a soup like this, so be sure to use the exact measurements given the first time you make it. I love this soup so much, I often use it as a sauce, too.

SERVES 6 TO 8

2 red onions, diced

6 cloves garlic

3 russet potatoes, peeled and diced

2 poblano chiles

1 red bell pepper, lightly roasted, seeded, and diced with skin on (page 121)

2 tablespoons olive oil

3 teaspoons salt

1 teaspoon freshly ground black pepper

1 gallon chicken stock (page 116)

1 tablespoon minced fresh epazote

1 pound fresh, frozen, or canned huitlacoche (thawed if frozen)

8 sprigs cilantro

1/2 cup sour cream

1. Preheat the oven on its highest setting.

2. In a large mixing bowl, combine the onions, garlic, potatoes, poblanos, bell pepper, olive oil, salt, and pepper. Toss well, transfer to a baking sheet, and place in the oven. Roast 15 to 20 minutes, then remove from the oven and turn with a spatula. Return to the oven and continue to roast until the onions, potatoes, and peppers are evenly charred around the edges. Set aside to cool.

3. In a large stockpot over high heat, bring the stock to a boil. Add the epazote and roasted onion-potato mixture. Add the huitlacoche and let boil for 15 minutes. Decrease the heat and simmer for 20 minutes.

4. Purée with a handheld blender until smooth.

5. Strip the cilantro leaves from the stems. Discard the stems and finely chop the leaves.

6. Ladle the soup into bowls. Sprinkle cilantro over the soup, add a dollop of sour cream to each, and serve.

sopa de garbanzos y camarones secos
[garbanzo bean and dried shrimp soup]

You might have a hard time finding dried shrimp. Look for them in Asian and Latin markets. Sometimes they are sold whole, and sometimes in a flour or powder form. Before modern methods of food transportation made virtually every food available all the time, shrimp were dried and stored for times when fresh were scarce. Like other dried foods, their flavor is much stronger than when fresh. Make sure you soak the garbanzo beans overnight. If you don't, they'll take much longer to cook than I've called for.

SERVES 6

8 ounces dried shrimp

10 ounces black garbanzo beans, soaked in water overnight and drained

2 bay leaves

1 gallon water

3 tablespoons achiote oil

1 white onion, diced

4 cloves garlic, diced

1 red bell pepper, diced

3 ounces cachucha chiles, stemmed, seeded, deribbed, and coarsely chopped

5 jalapeño chiles, stemmed and diced (including seeds)

1 tablespoon tomato paste

1 cup white wine

4 plum tomatoes, diced

2 limes, quartered

1. In a dry skillet over medium heat, toast the shrimp for 3 minutes. Turn out onto a plate and let cool. Using a food processor or a mortar and pestle, grind half of the toasted shrimp into a fine powder. Set aside.

2. In a large stockpot over medium heat, bring the remaining whole toasted shrimp, the garbanzo beans, bay leaves, and water to a simmer. Cover and cook 1 hour, then uncover.

3. Heat the oil in a sauté pan over high heat and sauté the onion, garlic, and peppers 5 minutes. Add the tomato paste and wine, and stir to combine.

4. Add the sauté mixture, tomatoes, and dried shrimp powder to the stockpot. Let simmer 20 more minutes.

5. Ladle the soup into bowls. Serve with the lime wedges on the side. Squeeze lime juice over the soup before eating.

sopa de habas
[fava bean soup]

A few years ago, I got to participate in a guest chef series at the finest hotel in Santiago, Chile. It was during fava bean season, and while taking a tour of the kitchen, I noticed that they had about ten employees peeling a big batch of fresh fava beans. Favas are so expensive here in the States, and so labor-intensive to prepare, that I immediately asked what they were using them for. They were making a soup for the employee cafeteria! Back at Patria, it would be considered ostentatious for us to make a staff meal out of fava beans, but favas are plentiful in Chile and no one seems to mind taking the time to prepare them. That week in Santiago inspired me to make this fava bean soup, but I've stretched the favas by adding fresh green peas. I also added bacon because its smoky flavor is the ideal match for the favas' mellow, earthy taste. If you wish to make this a vegetarian soup, you can omit the bacon and substitute vegetable stock or miso for the chicken stock. And this is a great soup for another reason: the leftovers taste just as good straight out of the refrigerator the next day. I love the soup hot, but I like it even more cold.

SERVES 4 TO 6

3 pounds fava beans, shelled

10 ounces applewood-smoked bacon, diced

1 white onion, diced

6 cloves garlic, chopped

1 gallon chicken stock (page 116)

2 potatoes, peeled and cut into large dice

2 cups heavy cream

1 cup fresh or frozen peas

1. Bring a large saucepan of water to a boil. Add the fava beans and blanch for 30 seconds, then drain. When cool enough to handle, slit the outer skin of the favas with the tip of a paring knife and slip out the beans. Set aside.

2. In a large stockpot over medium heat, stir and cook the bacon until it starts to crisp, 5 to 7 minutes. Add the onion and garlic, and cook 3 more minutes. Add the stock and potatoes, and increase the heat to medium-high. Bring to a boil and continue to boil for 12 minutes.

3. Decrease the heat to low, add the cream, favas, and peas and simmer briefly. Once the soup is simmering, purée it with a handheld blender until smooth.

4. Immediately ladle the soup into bowls and serve.

Locro de papas

sopad de mango, jengibre,
y Limon verde

crema de abune

sopa de guisantes
y jengibre

sopa de ajo

sopa de yuca

sopa de palmitos

sopa de boniato frío

gazpacho

ponche

caldo de bolas

sopa de aguacate

sopa de zapallo

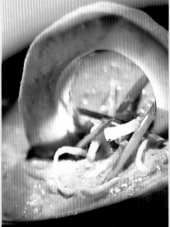

vegetable-
and fruit-based
soups

sopa de membrillo

sopa de hinojo

sopa poderosa

sopa de tomatillos
y coliflor

guiso de chayote

ajiaco de hongos

sopa de plátano

sopa de cebollita

Locro de papas
[creamy peasant-style potato soup]

Locro is a very simple, peasant-style soup that always has potatoes in it. There are many kinds of locros; this happens to be one of my favorites. Make sure to use gold potatoes, as the Ecuadoreans do.

SERVES 4

> *2 tablespoons vegetable oil*
> *2 white onions, diced*
> *3 garlic cloves*
> *3 quarts chicken stock (page 116)*
> *2 pounds Yukon gold potatoes, peeled and cut into 1-inch chunks*
> *1 12.5-ounce can evaporated milk*
> *³/₄ pound queso blanco, diced*

1. Heat the oil in a large stockpot over high heat. Add the onions and sauté 3 minutes. Add the garlic and stir. Add the stock and potatoes and bring to a boil. Decrease the heat and simmer for 30 to 40 minutes.

2. Stir in the evaporated milk and simmer 10 more minutes.

3. Stir in the cheese, then immediately ladle the soup into bowls and serve.

sopa de mango, jengibre, y Limón verde
[mango, ginger, and lime soup]

My mom has prolific avocado and mango trees in her backyard, and at one point she had more mangos than she could give away. I gladly took them and created this soup. The flavors really work well together; I've also used this flavor combination in a sorbet and many other items. This soup can be served as an appetizer or a dessert.

SERVES 4

> *2 pounds ripe mangos*
> *4 ounces fresh ginger, peeled*
> *4 cups mango nectar*
> *³/₄ cup freshly squeezed lime juice*

1. Peel and dice the mangos, discarding the pit.

2. Using a juice extractor, juice the mangos and ginger, adding the mango nectar 1 cup at a time.

3. Strain the liquid. Stir in the lime juice and refrigerate.

4. Ladle the ice-cold soup into bowls and serve.

CReMa ðe aBUNe
[CReam of ceLeRy Root soup]

Celery root is a tuber known as celeriac in the United States and *abune* in Venezuela, where I tasted a soup that inspired this recipe. Celery root has a more pungent flavor than standard celery and a slightly bitter aftertaste. Sweating and sautéing it in butter takes away some of that bitterness and leaves the intense celery taste. I've taken the liberty of adding dark rum to this soup—a nontraditional addition that gives the soup a sweet vanillalike flavor and helps cut the sharpness of the celery root. This is a great first course.

SERVES 4

$^1/_4$ cup (3 ounces) sweet butter
1 white onion, cut into small dice
$1^1/_2$ cups celeriac
3 stalks celery
4 cloves garlic, diced
1 potato, cut into large dice
3 tablespoons flour
1 gallon chicken stock (page 116)

3 bay leaves
Salt
Freshly ground black pepper
1 cup dark rum
1 cup heavy cream
Smoked Gouda cheese, finely grated

1. In a large 8-quart stockpot over high heat, sauté the butter, onion, celeriac, celery, garlic, and potato. Sprinkle the flour over the mixture and stir well. Add the stock, stir, and bring to a boil. Decrease the heat, add the bay leaves, and simmer for 1 hour.

2. Season to taste with salt and pepper and add the rum. Purée with a handheld blender or in batches in a bender. Add the cream and stir until evenly incorporated.

3. Ladle the soup into bowls. Sprinkle some of the cheese over each bowl and serve.

sopa de guisantes y jengibre
[sweet pea and ginger soup]

I love this soup. Sweet peas and ginger are a great combination—I also make a sweet pea and ginger flan and a rice dish—and the shocking color is a knock-out. One of my best soup-making secrets is the way I get green soups to have an electrifying color. For this one, I purée in the peas just before serving instead of letting them cook along with the other ingredients. Try it, and you'll see how this trick gives the soup an amazing color. When garden-fresh peas aren't in season, frozen peas will work just fine.

SERVES 4

3 tablespoons sweet butter
1 large white onion, diced
4 cloves garlic, minced
3 ounces fresh ginger, peeled and grated
2 tablespoons flour
1 gallon chicken stock
2 cups heavy cream
2 1/2 pounds fresh or frozen peas, shelled

1. In a large stockpot over medium heat, melt the butter. Add the onion, garlic, and ginger and sauté, while stirring continuously, about 6 minutes. Add the flour and continue to stir until it coats the onion evenly. Cook 3 more minutes. Add the stock and cream and stir well. Bring to a boil, then decrease the heat and simmer. Cook 20 minutes.

2. Add the peas and partially purée the mixture with a handheld blender, leaving chunks of onion and peas. Remove the soup from the heat and let sit 10 minutes.

3. Ladle the soup into bowls and serve.

sopa de ajo
[garlic soup]

Every Latin American country has a different version of a garlic soup, probably directly or indirectly inspired by the garlic-heavy dishes of classical spanish cuisine. This particular one is very easy to make—just be sure to eat it with friends!

SERVES 4

1 large white onion, diced

2 tablespoons butter, softened

1 large potato, peeled and diced (about 1 cup)

1 teaspoon Colman's mustard powder

1 teaspoon ground mace

1 gallon chicken stock (page 116)

$^1/_2$ cup olive oil

25 cloves garlic, chopped

8 ounces dried bread cubes

1 quart heavy cream

1. In a large stockpot over medium heat, sauté the onion in the butter for about 5 minutes, stirring often. Add the potato, mustard, and mace and continue to cook for 5 minutes. Add the stock and bring the mixture to a boil. Reduce the heat to a simmer and let simmer about 30 minutes.

2. Heat the oil in a sauté pan over high heat. Add the garlic to the hot oil and stir quickly, cooking until golden, but not beginning to brown, about 6 minutes. Pour the garlic into the stockpot and add the bread cubes and cream. Cook 10 more minutes. Purée with a handheld blender until smooth.

3. Ladle the soup into bowls and serve.

sopa de yuca
[yuca soup]

The finest yucas in the world come from Costa Rica. Yuca is one of those rare ingredients that can oxidize through its skin, similar to the way potatoes oxidize and turn brown shortly after they're peeled. One way to be sure you buy the freshest, nonoxidized yucas is to buy those that are waxed, which blocks oxidation. This soup is also good cold, like a vichyssoise.

SERVES 6

> 2 white onions, peeled and diced
>
> 2 small leeks, white part only, rinsed well and sliced
>
> 3 tablespoons butter
>
> 1 teaspoon mace
>
> 2 pounds yuca, peeled, split, strawlike center discarded, and diced
>
> 1 gallon chicken stock (page 116)
>
> 1 pint heavy cream

MOJO

> 1 cup flat-leaf parsley
>
> 4 cloves garlic, diced
>
> $1/2$ cup olive oil
>
> 3 tablespoons freshly squeezed lime juice
>
> 1 red onion, peeled and finely diced
>
> Salt and freshly ground black pepper

1. Place the onions and leeks in the bowl of a food processor and pulse a few times, then let the machine run until finely puréed, about 20 seconds. Set aside.

2. In a large stockpot over medium heat, melt the butter and sauté the puréed onion mixture about 10 minutes, stirring often. Add the mace, yuca, and stock, increase the heat to high, and bring to a boil. Decrease the heat to low, cover, and let simmer for 35 minutes.

3. Add the cream and purée the soup with a handheld blender. Strain the soup through a fine-mesh strainer. Return the soup to the stockpot and keep warm.

4. To make the mojo, place the parsley and garlic in the bowl of a miniature food processor and pulse until finely chopped. Whisk together the oil and lime juice. Add the puréed mixture and the red onion. Season to taste with salt and pepper.

5. Ladle the soup into bowls and serve with the mojo on the side. Spoon some of the mojo into the center of the soup, then eat.

sopa de palmitos
[hearts of palm soup]

It was illegal to bring fresh hearts of palm into the States until three or four years ago. Until, that is, a Costa Rican farmer approached me at Yuca in Miami, where I was chef at the time, and said he was the one who grew the enormous amount of yuca I was buying from the restaurant's produce supplier. He invited me to come see his farm, and so I went to Costa Rica. While there, I noticed that he grew hearts of palm, and I asked him what he did with the crop. He sold it all for canning. Somehow I convinced him to start importing hearts of palm hidden inside the boxes of yuca for me. Eventually, they became popular enough to be certified as an importable crop. I was one of the first chefs in the country to have fresh hearts of palm. Now they're readily available. I've even seen them in the local supermarket. I love fresh hearts of palm, and this soup is a great way to have them.

SERVES 4

6 ounces salt pork, skin discarded, cut into small dice

1 white onion, diced

2 leeks, white part only, rinsed well and sliced

1 tablespoon flour

1 gallon chicken stock (page 116)

1 turnip, peeled and diced (about 1 cup)

2 pounds fresh hearts of palm, sliced crosswise $^1/_2$ inch thick

1 cup heavy cream

Salt and freshly ground black pepper

1. Heat the salt pork in a large stockpot over medium heat while stirring. Let render about 10 minutes. Remove and discard the chunks. Add the onion and leeks to the fat, increase the heat to medium-high, and cook about 10 minutes. Add the flour and stir until it coats the onion and leeks evenly. Add the stock, increase the heat to high, and bring to a boil. Add the turnip and hearts of palm. Decrease the heat to low, cover and simmer for 20 minutes.

2. Add the cream and simmer 10 minutes. Purée the soup with a handheld blender. Season to taste with the salt and pepper.

3. Ladle the soup into bowls and serve.

sopa de boniato frío
[chilled boniato soup]

Here's another Latin American–style
vichyssoise, which can easily be convert-
ed to a vegetarian soup by substituting
vegetable stock for the chicken stock. The
recipe was inspired by a soup I used to
make with yuca. I was experimenting
with various tubers, and boniato became
one of my favorites. The peppery ginger
adds a nice zing and balances the sweet
boniato. I like to eat this soup as the first
course in a light lunch.

Serves 4

3 tablespoons olive oil

1 small white onion, diced

*3 ounces fresh ginger, peeled
   and diced*

2 pounds boniato, peeled and cubed

2 cups chicken stock (page 116)

$1/2$ teaspoon ground mace

$1^1/2$ cups chilled heavy cream

Salt and freshly ground black pepper

Boniato Chips (page 114)

1. In a heavy-bottomed stockpot, heat the
   olive oil over medium heat. Add the
   onion and cook until transparent. Add
   the ginger, boniato, and stock. Increase
   the heat to medium-high and bring the
   mixture to a boil.

2. Once the mixture is boiling, decrease the
   heat to low and simmer for 30 minutes.

3. Add the mace and remove from the
   heat. Let cool on the stovetop for about
   $1^1/2$ hours.

4. When the soup is cool, purée with a
   handheld blender. Add the cream and stir
   until evenly incorporated. Season with
   salt and pepper, then cover and refrigerate to thicken overnight.

5. Ladle ice cold soup into bowls and serve
   with the boniato chips on the side.

gazpacho
[vegetable soup]

I once gave a recipe for gazpacho to a talented young chef named Manny Mercado, who was working for me at Yuca. He "Manny-ized" the soup by adding yellow peppers, lime juice, and garlic, then puréeing the ingredients to make it supersmooth. It's a refreshing interpretation of an old standard.

SERVES 4

12 ripe plum tomatoes, peeled and diced (page 121)

3 tablespoons freshly squeezed lime juice

3 cloves garlic

3 tablespoons Tabasco sauce

2 jalapeño peppers, stemmed and diced (including seeds)

1 cup water

12 cucumbers, peeled and diced

1 red bell pepper, cut into small dice

1 yellow bell pepper, cut into small dice

1 red onion, diced

4 green onions, sliced

5 sprigs cilantro, leaves removed and stems discarded

1/4 cup olive oil

Salt and pepper to taste

1. In a blender, combine the tomatoes, lime juice, garlic, Tabasco, jalapeños, and water and blend until smooth.

2. Add the cucumber, bell peppers, onion, green onions, cilantro leaves, and oil and blend well. Season to taste with salt and pepper.

3. Cover and refrigerate until thoroughly chilled.

4. Ladle into bowls and serve.

ponche
[chilled exotica fruit soup]

I enjoy this soup several ways: as a dessert, a starter for a light meal, or a smoothielike drink. But unlike any other tropical fruit blend you've had before, this one has a fabulous (or fabutastic!, as I like to say) flavor that comes from mixing the tart fruits and spicy allspice, cloves, and peppercorns. The rum brings out the flavors of each fruit.

SERVES 6

3 cups light rum

1 pineapple, peeled, cored, and diced

2 green apples, peeled, cored, and diced

2 papayas, peeled and diced

2 mangoes, peeled, seeded, and diced

6 passion fruit, seeded and flesh scooped out of skin

4 cups freshly squeezed orange juice

8 whole cloves

10 allspice berries

25 black peppercorns

3 vanilla beans

1 small bunch green grapes

2 to 3 bananas

1. In an 8-quart stockpot over high heat, combine all the soup ingredients except the vanilla beans and bring to a boil.

2. When the soup is boiling, decrease the heat to low and simmer for about 1 hour.

3. Remove the soup from the heat and let cool in the stockpot. (This step is important; it allows the ingredients to infuse the soup with their full flavors.)

4. When the soup is completely cool, purée in a blender or with a handheld blender. Pour the soup through a fine-mesh strainer and discard the cloves, allspice berries, and peppercorns.

5. Slice the vanilla beans open lengthwise and scrape out the pulp into the soup. Stir to incorporate evenly.

6. Cover the soup and refrigerate until ice cold. Slice the grapes in half and cut the bananas into thin slices. Ladle the soup into bowls and garnish each with a few grape halves and slices of banana.

caldo de bolas
[roasted vegetable soup
with plantain dumplings]

I like to call this an Ecuadorean-style matzo ball soup because the balls are made with plantains. Traditionally, the balls are filled with pork and cooked in a pork broth, but I created this version specifically to serve as a vegetarian special at Patria. It's almost like a stewed cabbage dish, but every once in a while when you take a bite, you get a raisin or olive or caper, so it has a nice contrast of sweet and salty. You can be creative and make a different filling if you like. I've made it with one big dumpling stuffed with a duck filling and cooked in duck broth, then ladled into bowls lined with sliced duck breast. Now that's a rich dish.

SERVES 6 TO 8

3 tablespoons plus 1 tablespoon achiote oil (page 115)

1 white onion, diced

1 red bell pepper, diced

2 cloves garlic

2 tablespoons raisins

2 tablespoons capers

$1/4$ cup dark rum

2 cups diced green cabbage

2 tablespoons ground ancho chile powder

1 teaspoon ground chipotle chile powder

2 tablespoons tomato paste

$1/4$ cup kalamata olives, chopped

2 cups plum tomatoes, diced

1 bunch fresh thyme

5 sprigs cilantro, leaves removed and stems discarded

3 sprigs flat-leaf parsley, leaves removed and stems discarded

1 gallon vegetable stock (page 120)

1 bay leaf

4 large green plantains, peeled

Salt

1. To make the filling, heat the oil in a large sauté pan over high heat. Add the onion, bell pepper, garlic, raisins, and capers. Sauté for 5 minutes. Add the rum and cook until the alcohol evaporates, about 3 minutes. Add the cabbage, stir and cook 3 minutes. Add the chile powders, tomato paste, olives, tomatoes, thyme, cilantro and parsley leaves, and stir until paste is well mixed. Cook 2 more minutes. Transfer the mixture to a mixing bowl and let cool.

2. Bring one-half of the stock and the bay leaf to a boil in a large stockpot over high heat. Add the whole plantains, decrease the heat to low, and simmer for 35 to 40 minutes, or until plantains are tender. Remove the plantains with a strainer and set aside.

3. Line a tray with waxed paper. Place 1 plantain, 1 teaspoon of achiote oil, and a pinch of salt in the bowl of a food processor. Process about 30 seconds, or until the plantain is completely smooth. Working very quickly, spread 2 tablespoons of the mixture in one cupped hand. Place 2 tablespoons of filling in the center and carefully shape the plantain mixture around the filling. Knead gently to form a ball and set on the tray to rest. Repeat with the remaining plantains and filling.

4. Bring the remaining stock to a simmer. Add the plantain balls and season to taste with salt. Simmer for 8 to 10 minutes.

5. Ladle the soup into bowls and serve immediately.

sopa de aguacate
[avocado soup]

I've made this soup with several different kinds of avocados, but nothing beats the richness and flavor of the California Haas variety. You can serve the soup cold, but I prefer to eat it at room temperature because when you chill the soup, the fat tightens up and holds back some of the avocado flavor. The chicken stock is optional; you may substitute vegetable stock, or even water, if you prefer. The tomatillos perk up the soup, and the cilantro adds spark as well. This is a nice one to start off a meal with.

SERVES 6

2 tablespoons olive oil

1 white onion, diced

5 jalapeño peppers, including seeds

3 cloves garlic

6 ounces green tomatillos, husked and rinsed in warm water

2 quarts chicken stock (page 116)

$1/2$ cup tightly packed cilantro leaves

7 ripe Haas avocados, peeled and pitted

Juice of 4 limes

1 lemon

1 bunch green onions, green parts only, cut into 2-inch lengths

1. Heat the oil in a large stockpot over medium heat. Add the the onion, jalapeños, garlic, and tomatillos and sauté. Add the stock and bring to a boil, then decrease the heat and simmer 20 minutes. Remove the pot from the heat and let sit for 1 hour, or until room temperature.

2. With a handheld blender, purée the ingredients until smooth. Add the cilantro, 6 of the avocados, and the lime juice. Purée again until smooth.

3. Zest the lemon and slice the remaining avocado. Ladle the soup into bowls and garnish with the zest, green onions, and avocado slices.

sopa de zapallo
[roasted acorn squash soup]

Zapallo is the Chilean word for a type of calabaza. This soup is unique because it's made with a roasted, blackened acorn squash. The black specks of caramelized squash in the soup create a great visual effect, so make sure to roast it until it's really black all over. The freshly grated ginger and chipotle chile powder are my additions to this Chilean recipe. Once you've roasted the squash, the rest of the soup is actually quite simple to make.

SERVES 4 TO 6

3 pounds zapallo or acorn squash, seeded, peeled, and diced

1 large white onion, cut into large dice

2 tablespoons sweet butter, melted

2 teaspoons ground allspice

1 teaspoon salt

1 teaspoon freshly ground black pepper

1 teaspoon chipotle chile powder

1 ounce fresh ginger, peeled and grated

1 gallon chicken stock (page 116)

1 cup heavy cream

1 russet potato, peeled and diced

5 cloves garlic

Shelled pumpkin seeds, toasted (page 121)

1. Move the oven rack to the highest position. Preheat the broiler or oven on its highest setting.

2. In a large mixing bowl, combine the zapallo or acorn squash, onion, butter, allspice, salt, pepper, chile powder, and ginger. Transfer to a baking sheet and cook in the oven for 10 minutes. Remove, turn ingredients with a metal spatula, and cook another 10 minutes, or until they are evenly charred. Set aside to cool.

3. In a large stockpot over high heat, combing the stock, cream, potato, and garlic. Bring to a boil, let boil 10 minutes, then decrease the heat to low and simmer for 30 minutes.

4. Add the charred vegetables to the stockpot. Purée with a handheld blender until completely smooth.

5. Ladle the soup into bowls. Sprinkle some of the pumpkin seeds over the soup and serve.

sopa de membrillo
[quince soup]

Quince is one of the oldest fruits around, and it contains a lot of pectin, a natural thickener like gelatin. When this soup gets cold, it gels and gets even thicker than it did while cooking. I like to add a little bit of apple juice to it because the sweetness enhances the quince's tartness. It's a very simple soup and a great starter for a summer meal.

SERVES 4

> *3 pounds quince, peeled, cored, and chopped*
> *Zest and juice of 3 lemons*
> *1 cup sugar*
> *1 teaspoon ground mace*
> *$1/2$ teaspoon ground cloves*
> *2 cups unfiltered apple juice*
> *2 quarts water*

1. In a medium stockpot over very low heat, combine all ingredients and simmer uncovered for 2 hours.

2. Turn off the heat and cool for 1 hour.

3. Purée the soup with a handheld blender.

4. Strain the soup through a fine-meshed strainer, discarding any pulp and solids. Cover and refrigerate until ice cold.

5. Ladle the soup into bowls and serve.

sopa de hinojo
[fennel soup]

I added Pernod, an anise-flavored French liqueur, to this soup to bring out the flavor of the fennel. You could also use *aguardiente*, a lighter Colombian liqueur.

SERVES 6

> *2 tablespoons sweet butter, softened*
> *1 cup Pernod*
> *6 bulbs fennel, cut crosswise into $1/2$-inch-thick slices, tops reserved*
> *2 white onions, diced*
> *6 cloves garlic, chopped*
> *1 gallon chicken stock (page 116)*
> *Salt*
> *Freshly ground black pepper*
> *2 cups heavy cream*

1. In a large stockpot over medium heat, melt the butter. Add $1/2$ cup of the Pernod, the fennel, onions, and garlic. Stir and cook about 5 minutes. Add the stock, increase the heat to medium-high and bring to a boil. Decrease the heat to low and simmer 15 minutes. Purée the soup with a handheld blender. Cook 10 more minutes. Season to taste with salt and pepper. Add the cream and cook another 10 minutes.

2. Ladle the soup into bowls. Garnish with some of the fennel leaves from the tops of the bulbs, and serve.

sopa poderosa
[power soup]

This soup requires a fair amount of labor because you have to roast all the vegetables, but it's worth the effort. Roasting brings out the vegetables' natural sweetness and means they only need to be simmered in the broth for a few minutes. We call it Power Soup because my friend who invented it, and former employee Ramon Madrano, swore it was an aphrodisiac. The soup is a favorite at Patria. I serve it with a smoked fish salad on the side and a wedge of lime. It's a complete meal, and it's excellent.

SERVES 6

> 3 jalapeño peppers, stemmed and diced (including seeds)
>
> 3 red bell peppers, diced
>
> 2 yellow bell peppers, diced
>
> 1 white onion, peeled and diced
>
> 4 tomatoes, diced
>
> 4 Red Bliss potatoes, diced
>
> 1 teaspoon pulverized garlic (with a mortar and pestle)
>
> 2 quarts fish stock (page 117)
>
> 3 green onions, white and green parts sliced (about $1/2$ cup)
>
> 1 bunch chives, minced
>
> Dash of sherry
>
> 10 sprigs cilantro, leaves removed and stems discarded
>
> 2 limes, quartered

1. Preheat the oven to 350°. Lightly coat a roasting pan with olive oil. Combine the jalapeños, bell peppers, onion, tomatoes, potatoes, and garlic and place in the roasting pan. Roast vegetables in oven for 35 minutes, or until tender but not blackened.

2. In a medium stockpot over medium heat, bring the stock to a simmer. Add the green onions, chives, and sherry, and simmer for 20 minutes.

3. Approximately 35 minutes before serving the soup, chop the cilantro leaves and stir into the soup.

4. Ladle into bowls and serve with the lime wedges on the side. Squeeze lime juice over the soup before eating.

sopa de tomatillos y coliflor
[tomatillo and cauliflower soup]

Central Americans often cook with cauliflower, but they don't usually make soup with it. Most commonly, they pickle it with vinegar and serve it as an accompaniment for all kinds of dishes. This recipe is very interesting because it calls for roasting the cauliflower, which gives it a completely different flavor than we're all used to. I like to keep this soup as green as possible, and that's why I purée in the spinach at the very end.

SERVES 4

> *2 heads cauliflower, trimmed and cut into florets*
> *1 white onion, diced*
> *4 cloves garlic, minced*
> *3 tablespoons sweet butter, softened*
> *2 tablespoons olive oil*
> *10 ounces tomatillos, husked and rinsed in warm water*
> *5 jalapeño peppers, including seeds, stemmed and sliced*
> *1 gallon chicken stock (page 116)*
> *8 ounces fresh spinach, stems removed, rinsed and chopped*
> *$^{1}/_{2}$ cup tightly packed cilantro leaves*
> *Salt*
> *$^{1}/_{2}$ cup sour cream*

1. Place a rack in the highest position and preheat the oven broiler.

2. Combine the cauliflower, onion, garlic, and butter in a mixing bowl. Transfer the cauliflower mixture to a baking sheet and broil for 10 minutes, or until the edges of the florets are blackened. Set aside to cool.

3. In a large pot over high heat, sauté the oil, tomatillos, and jalapeños for 5 minutes, stirring often. Add the stock, bring to a boil, let boil 5 minutes, then decrease the heat and simmer.

4. Add the spinach and cilantro and let simmer 10 minutes. Add the cauliflower. Purée with a handheld blender until smooth. Season to taste with salt. Let simmer 5 minutes.

5. Ladle the soup into bowls. Garnish with a dollop of sour cream and serve.

guiso de chayote
[chayote stew]

Guiso translates into "stew," and this one is infused with a delicate chicken flavor. Chayote doesn't have a lot of flavor; its primary purpose is to add texture and substance. Its flesh is like a cross between a cucumber and squash. It's sort of pear shaped, and it absorbs the flavor of whatever it's cooked with, although many think it's an acquired taste.

SERVES 4 TO 6

1 gallon chicken stock (page 116)

2 skinless, boneless chicken breasts

2 russet potatoes, peeled and julienned with a mandoline

2 tablespoons butter

1 large white onion, diced

6 chayotes, peeled and julienned

6 cloves garlic

1 teaspoon ground chipotle chile powder

2 teaspoons ground ancho chile powder

1 pint heavy cream

2 tablespoons red wine vinegar

2 tablespoons olive oil

Salt and freshly ground black pepper

2 large red onions, diced

1 bunch green onions, white and green parts, sliced

1 bunch chives, sliced

1 cup sour cream

1. Place the stock and chicken breasts in a stockpot. Bring to a simmer over low heat, then cover and let simmer for 35 minutes. Remove the chicken breasts and let cool. Keep stock simmering and add the potatoes.

2. Heat the butter in a sauté pan over high heat. Add the white onion, half of the chayotes, and the garlic and sauté for 5 minutes. Stir in the chile powders and cook for 5 more minutes. Set aside.

3. When the chicken is cool, shred it, using one fork to anchor the meat and the other to tear it off the breast into small strips.

4. Add the cream, chayote mixture, and chicken to the stockpot and let simmer for 10 minutes.

5. Meanwhile, whisk together the red wine vinegar, olive oil, salt, and pepper in a large mixing bowl. Add the remaining chayotes, red onions, green onions, and chives and toss to coat evenly.

6. Place a generous amount of the chayote and onion mixture in each soup bowl. Ladle the soup over and serve with a dollop of sour cream on the side.

ajiaco дe HONGOS
[musHROOm stew]

My inventive sous chef Andrew DiCataldo created this fabulous version of a soup that's usually made with various meats. He had the brilliant idea to use Latin American tubers to achieve the "meatiness" of the traditional soup without the heaviness of the meats. It's very popular at Patria during the winter.

SERVES 6

5 tablespoons achiote oil

1 large onion, diced (about 1 cup)

2 teaspoons pulverized garlic (with a mortar and pestle)

1 1/2 gallons vegetable stock (page 120)

1 large yuca, halved, peeled, center strings removed, then diced (about 1 cup)

6 ounces boniato, peeled and diced (about 1/2 cup)

8 ounces calabaza, peeled and diced (about 1 cup)

1/2 large malanga, diced (about 1/2 cup)

1/2 teaspoon salt

1 teaspoon freshly ground black pepper

2 tablespoons dark miso

1 large russet potato, diced (about 1 cup)

2 ears corn, shucked and cut crosswise into pinwheels

8 ounces sliced shiitake mushrooms (about 2 cups)

4 ounces sliced cremini mushrooms (about 1 cup)

4 ounces wild mushrooms (about 1 cup)

3 ounces dried morels, rehydrated in 1/4 cup brandy and 1/4 cup port

2 sprigs flat-leaf parsley

White truffle oil

1. Heat 3 tablespoons of the achiote oil in a stockpot over high heat. Add the onion and garlic and sauté for 3 minutes.

2. Add the stock, yuca, boniato, calabaza, malanga, salt, pepper, and miso. Bring to a boil, then add the potato and corn. Decrease the heat to low, cover, and simmer for 45 minutes, stirring occasionally.

3. Heat the remaining 2 tablespoons of oil in a large saute pan over high heat. Add the shiitakes, creminis, and wild mushrooms and cook 5 minutes, stirring continuously. Drain off any excess liquid and slice the mushrooms. Return pan to the heat, add the brandy and morels, and cook for 5 minutes while stirring. Add the mushrooms to the stockpot and stir to incorporate well.

4. Just before serving, chop the parsley.

5. Ladle the soup into bowls. Sprinkle parsley over the top of the soup, drizzle with truffle oil, and serve.

sopa de plátano
[green plantain soup]

Green plantain-based soups are popular in Puerto Rico and in Cuba, and this one was always a favorite in my house when I was growing up. The broth was heavily spiced with aromatics like Cuban coriander. I've spiced up mom's recipe with the mustard seeds, crushed red pepper, and ginger. If you don't want to make your own plantain flour, just pick up some at a Latin market and substitute 1 cup for the 2 green plantains and canola oil.

SERVES 6 TO 8

- *1 gallon water*
- *2 pounds skirt or flank steak, well trimmed*
- *1 small white onion, peeled and diced*
- *1 carrot, peeled and diced*
- *3 cloves garlic*
- *4 bay leaves*
- *1 tablespoon oregano*
- *1 teaspoon thyme*
- *1 teaspoon cumin seeds*
- *1 tablespoon peppercorns*
- *1 tablespoon mustard seeds*
- *1 ounce fresh ginger, peeled and grated*
- *1 teaspoon ground coriander*
- *1 cinnamon stick*
- *1 tablespoon crushed red pepper flakes*

ROPA VIEJA

- *3 tablespoons olive oil*
- *1 small white onion, peeled and julienned*
- *1/2 red bell pepper, julienned (about 1/2 cup)*
- *1/2 yellow bell pepper, julienned (about 1/2 cup)*
- *1 teaspoon pulverized garlic (with mortar and pestle)*
- *3 plum tomatoes, diced*
- *1/2 teaspoon salt*
- *3/4 teaspoon freshly ground black pepper*
- *1/2 cup dry sherry*
- *1/4 cup dry white wine*
- *2 teaspoons tomato paste*

———

- *2 green plantains, peeled and sliced*
- *Canola oil*
- *1 green plantain, peeled and diced (page 121)*
- *1 sweet plantain, peeled and diced*
- *5 cloves garlic*

1. Combine the water and next 14 ingredients in a stockpot over high heat. Bring to a boil and continue to boil for 5 minutes. Decrease the heat to low, cover, and simmer for 30 minutes. Strain, reserving the broth and meat and discarding the

vegetables and spices. Rinse the meat under cold running water in a colander for about 5 minutes. When cool enough to handle, shred the meat into long strands with two forks.

2. To make the ropa vieja, heat the oil in a large sauté pan over high heat. Add the onion, bell peppers, and garlic and sauté for 3 minutes. Add the meat, cook for 5 minutes, then add the tomatoes, salt, and pepper.

3. In a small bowl, combine the sherry and wine and stir in the tomato paste. Add to the saute pan, and cook for 4 minutes. Remove the pan from the heat and set aside.

4. Heat 1 inch of canola oil in a heavy-bottomed skillet over high heat. Add the sliced green plantains and fry until golden brown and crispy. Transfer to paper towels to drain. When cool, place in a plastic bag and crush. Place plantain chips in the bowl of a food processor and pulse until chips have turned into a flour-like powder. Measure out 1 cup of plantain flour and reserve the rest for another use.

5. In a stockpot, bring the strained stock to a boil over high heat. Add the ropa vieja mixture, the diced green and sweet plantains, and garlic. Boil for 10 minutes, then decrease the heat to low, cover and simmer for 30 minutes.

6. With a handheld blender puree the soup while adding $1/4$ cup plantain flour at a time, waiting until it is incorporated before pouring in the next addition.

7. Add the shredded meat and cook 15 minutes.

8. Ladle the soup into bowls and serve.

sopa de cebollita
[spanish onion soup]

This is based on a classical soup from Colombia, where they grow pearl onions. They use white pearl onions, but I prefer red ones because they're sweeter when cooked whole. I leave the ends of the onions attached because they're more striking that way. I've updated the soup by adding some sherry, blasamic vinegar, and soy sauce to the broth.

SERVES 4

- *3 tablespoons sweet butter*
- *2 red or white pearl onions, julienned*
- *1 cup dry sherry*
- *3 tablespoons Worcestershire sauce*
- *3 tablespoons soy sauce*
- *3 tablespoons balsamic vinegar*
- *1 gallon beef stock (page 115)*
- *1 pound skirt steak*
- *2 tablespoons flour*
- *6 cloves garlic, finely chopped*
- *1/2 teaspoon salt*
- *1/2 teaspoon freshly ground black pepper*
- *2 tablespoons olive oil*
- *3 pounds pearl onions, peeled*

1. In a large stockpot over high heat, melt the butter. Add the julienned onions and caramelize while stirring, about 6 minutes. Add the sherry, Worcestershire, soy, and balsamic. Reduce and cook about 10 minutes. Add the stock and bring to a boil, then decrease the heat to low, cover, and simmer.

2. Combine the flour, garlic, salt, and pepper in a large mixing bowl. Cut the steak into thin strips and toss with the flour mixture to coat evenly. Heat the oil in a sauté pan over high heat. Add the steak strips and sear while stirring for about 5 minutes.

3. Uncover the stockpot. Add the steak strips and simmer for about 20 minutes. Add the peeled onions and simmer another 20 minutes.

4. Ladle the soup into bowls and serve.

basics

cooked white rice

MAKES ABOUT 4 CUPS

> *2 cups long-grain white rice*
> *2$^1/_2$ tablespoons vegetable oil*
> *2 teaspoons salt*
> *2 quarts water*

1. Rinse the rice in a colander under cold running water until the water runs clear. Drain.

2. Place the rice, oil, salt, and water in a saucepan over medium-high heat and bring to a boil. Continue to boil, uncovered, until almost all of the water has cooked off, 10 to 12 minutes.

3. Stir the rice, cover, decrease the heat to low, and simmer for 8 to 10 minutes.

4. Remove the rice from the heat and fluff with a fork just before serving.

boniato chips

SERVES 4

> *3 cups canola oil*
> *2 large boniatos, peeled and finely sliced lengthwise*
> *Salt*
> *Ground cumin*

1. Heat the oil to 350° in a deep fryer or heavy-bottomed saucepan. Immediately add the boniato slices one at a time, taking care to leave at least 1 inch between slices. (If you overload the fryer or pan, the oil will not stay hot enough to properly fry the slices.) Deep-fry for 3 to 4 minutes, or until golden.

2. Remove the chips with a wire-mesh strainer and set on paper towels to drain. Immediately sprinkle with salt and cumin, then let cool completely as you continue to cook the remaining slices.

achiote oil

MAKES ABOUT $1^1/_2$ CUPS
> **1 cup vegetable oil**
> **$^1/_2$ cup annatto seeds**

1. Heat the oil and seeds in a saucepan over low heat just until the oil begins to bubble, 8 to 10 minutes. Remove the pan from the heat and let rest for 3 hours, or until the oil becomes infused with the annatto.

2. Pour the oil slowly into a glass container and discard the sediment at the bottom of the pan. Cover the oil tightly and store in the refrigerator for up to 6 months.

sofrito

MAKES ABOUT $1^1/_2$ CUPS
> **2 tablespoons achiote oil**
> **1 white onion, peeled and diced**
> **1 green bell pepper, seeded and diced**
> **1 tomato, diced**
> **5 cloves garlic, minced**

1. Heat the oil in a large sauté pan over high heat. Add the onion and bell pepper, and sauté 2 minutes. Add the tomato and garlic, and cook 5 minutes longer, or until the tomato pieces begin to lose their form and shape.

2. Let cool, then use as directed.

beef stock

MAKES ABOUT 1 GALLON
> **2 pounds skirt steak**
> **3 carrots, peeled and coarsely chopped**
> **1 white onion, cut into eighths**
> **3 stalks celery, coarsely chopped**
> **3 tablespoons pickling spice**
> **8 cloves garlic**
> **4 sprigs thyme**
> **6 sprigs flat-leaf parsley**
> **Water**

1. Place the skirt steak and all other ingredients in an 8-quart stockpot. Bring to a boil over medium-high heat. When the mixture is boiling, decrease the heat to low and simmer for 2 hours, periodically skimming off any fat and impurities that rise to the surface.

2. Remove the skirt steak from the stockpot and pour the liquid through a fine-mesh strainer. Discard the vegetables, herbs, and spices and use the stock and skirt steak as directed.

chicken stock

MAKES ABOUT 1 GALLON

- 2 pounds whole or cut-up chicken, including neck and wings, rinsed and patted dry
- 3 carrots, peeled and coarsely chopped
- 2 stalks celery, coarsely chopped
- 1 white onion, cut into eighths
- 1 clove garlic, halved
- 1 teaspoon dried thyme
- 10 sprigs cilantro
- 6 sprigs flat-leaf parsley
- 6 sprigs dill
- 1 tablespoon dried oregano
- 1 tablespoon whole black peppercorns
- Water

1. Place the chicken and all other ingredients in an 8-quart stockpot. Bring to a boil over medium-high heat. When the mixture is boiling, decrease the heat to low and simmer for 2 to 3 hours, periodically skimming off any fat and impurities that rise to the surface.

2. Remove the chicken from the stockpot and pour the liquid through a fine-mesh strainer. Remove the meat from the chicken carcass and use as directed. Discard the vegetables and peppercorns and use the stock as directed.

corn stock

MAKES ABOUT 3 QUARTS

- $1/2$ cup (4 ounces) sweet butter
- 10 corn cobs, cut into 1-inch-thick rounds
- 3 leeks, washed, split, and chopped (including some of the green tops)
- 1 white onion, cut into eighths
- 3 carrots, peeled and coarsely chopped
- 1 tablespoon saffron threads
- 1 gallon water
- 3 tablespoons whole black peppercorns
- 4 jalapeño chiles
- 3 tablespoons tomato paste
- 3 bay leaves
- 4 sprigs thyme

1. In a 6-quart stockpot over high medium, melt the butter. Add the corn cob pieces, leeks, onion, carrots, and saffron and sweat until softened and onion is translucent but not at all browned, 8 to 10 minutes. Add the water and the remaining ingredients, increase the heat to high, and bring to a boil. Decrease the heat to low and simmer for $1^1/2$ hours, periodically skimming off any fat and impurities that rise to the surface.

2. Pour the stock mixture through a fine-mesh strainer. Discard the vegetables and herbs and use the stock as directed.

Lobster stock

MAKES ABOUT 3 QUARTS

5 pounds lobster shells (or carcasses), split

1 cup (8 ounces) sweet butter

4 to 6 carrots, peeled and coarsely chopped

4 to 6 stalks celery, coarsely chopped

4 white onions, coarsely chopped

3 cloves garlic, halved

3 cups dry sherry

1 tablespoon crushed red pepper flakes

4 bay leaves

1 bunch thyme, tied with kitchen twine

1 bunch parsley, tied with kitchen twine

¼ cup tomato paste

1 gallon water

1. Thoroughly wash out the lobster shells, taking care to remove the lungs.

2. Melt the butter in a stockpot over high heat. Add the lobster shells, carrots, celery, onions, and garlic and sauté, stirring continuously until softened, about 20 minutes. Add the wine and deglaze the pot. Cook 5 more minutes.

3. Add the remaining ingredients and bring to a boil. When the mixture is boiling, decrease the heat to low and simmer for 2 hours, periodically skimming off any fat and impurities that rise to the surface.

4. Pour the liquid through a fine-mesh strainer. Discard the vegetables and herbs and use the stock as directed.

Fish stock

MAKES ABOUT 1 GALLON

2 pounds whitefish carcass (such as snapper or flounder), including bones

3 carrots, peeled and coarsely chopped

2 stalks celery, coarsely chopped

1 white onion, cut into eighths

1 tablespoon whole black peppercorns

6 sprigs flat-leaf parsley

4 sprigs thyme

Water

1. Place the fish carcass and all other ingredients in an 8-quart stockpot. Fill the stockpot with water and bring to a gentle simmer over medium heat. When the mixture is simmering, decrease the heat to low and simmer slowly for 1 hour, periodically skimming off any fat and impurities that rise to the surface.

2. Pour the stock mixture through a fine-mesh strainer. Discard the vegetables and herbs and use the stock as directed.

Ham stock

MAKES ABOUT 1 GALLON

  3 pounds ham hocks

  3 carrots, peeled and coarsely
    chopped

  2 stalks celery, coarsely chopped

  1 white onion, cut into eighths

  1 tablespoon whole black peppercorns

  8 cloves garlic

  3 to 4 bay leaves

  3 sprigs thyme

  3 plum tomatoes, quartered

  Water

1. Place the ham hocks and all other ingredients in an 8-quart stockpot. Fill the stockpot with water and bring to a boil over medium-high heat. When the mixture is boiling, decrease the heat to low and simmer for 3 to 4 hours, periodically skimming off any fat and impurities that rise to the surface.

2. Remove the ham hocks from the stockpot and pour the liquid through a fine-mesh strainer. Remove the meat from the ham hocks and use as directed. Discard the vegetables and peppercorns and use the stock as directed.

Roasted Chicken stock

MAKES ABOUT 1 GALLON

  1 tablespoon paprika

  2 tablespoons ground ancho
    chile powder

  3 tablespoons achiote oil (page 115)

  $1/2$ teaspoon salt

  1 teaspoon freshly ground
    black pepper

  2 pounds whole or cut-up chicken,
    including neck and wings,
    rinsed and patted dry

  3 carrots, peeled and coarsely
    chopped

  2 stalks celery, coarsely chopped

  1 white onion, cut into eighths

  3 bay leaves

  4 sprigs thyme

  1 tablespoon black peppercorns

  3 pieces chipotle chile

  1 tablespoon dried oregano

  1 tablespoon ground allspice

  3 whole cloves

  1 cinnamon stick

  Water

1. Preheat a grill.

2. In a bowl, combine the paprika, ancho chile powder, achiote oil, salt, and pepper. Add the chicken and toss to coat evenly. Grill the chicken briefly over high heat, just until char grill marks form and chicken is turning golden brown.

3. Transfer the seasoned chicken to an 8-quart stockpot and add the remaining ingredients. Fill the stockpot with water and bring to a boil over medium-high heat. When the mixture is boiling, decrease the heat to low and simmer for 2 to 3 hours, periodically skimming off any fat and impurities that rise to the surface.

4. Remove the chicken from the stockpot and pour the liquid through a fine-mesh strainer. Remove the meat from the chicken carcass and use as directed. Discard the vegetables and peppercorns and use the stock as directed.

sHrimp stock

MAKES ABOUT 1 GALLON

   1 cup (8 ounces) sweet butter
   2 pounds shrimp shells
   3 carrots, peeled and coarsely chopped
   2 stalks celery, coarsely chopped
   1 white onion, cut into eighths
   5 cloves garlic
   2 cups dry white wine
   2 cups brandy
   3 jalapeno chiles, stemmed and sliced (including seeds)
   1 tablespoon crushed red pepper flakes
   3 bay leaves
   4 sprigs thyme
   3 sprigs fresh parsley
   3 tablespoons tomato paste
   $1/2$ teaspoon salt
   1 teaspoon freshly ground black pepper
   Water

1. Melt the butter in an 8-quart stockpot over high heat. Add the shrimp shells, carrots, celery, onion, and garlic and sauté, stirring continuously until softened, about 20 minutes. Add the wine and brandy and deglaze the pot. Cook 5 more minutes.

2. Add the remaining ingredients, fill the stockpot with water and bring to a boil. When the mixture is boiling, decrease the heat to low and simmer for 2 hours, periodically skimming off any fat and impurities that rise to the surface.

3. Pour the liquid through a fine-mesh strainer. Discard the vegetables and herbs and use the stock as directed.

veal stock

MAKES ABOUT 1 GALLON

3 pounds meaty veal bones

3 carrots, peeled and coarsely chopped

1 white onion, cut into eighths

3 stalks celery, coarsely chopped

3 tablespoons pickling spice

8 cloves garlic

4 sprigs thyme

6 sprigs flat-leaf parsley

Water

1. Place the veal bones and all other ingredients in an 8-quart stockpot. Bring to a boil over medium-high heat. When the mixture is boiling, decrease the heat to low and simmer for 2 hours, periodically skimming off any fat and impurities that rise to the surface.

2. Pour the stock through a fine-mesh strainer. Discard the bones, vegetables, herbs, and spices and use the stock as directed.

vegetable stock

MAKES ABOUT 3 QUARTS

1 white onion, cut into eighths

3 leeks, washed, split, and chopped (including some green tops)

3 carrots, peeled and coarsely chopped

6 stalks celery, coarsely chopped

3 to 4 shallots, peeled and chopped (about $^1/_2$ cup)

6 cloves garlic, chopped

4 plum tomatoes, diced

6 sprigs thyme

4 bay leaves, crumbled

1 tablespoon black peppercorns

6 sprigs flat-leaf parsley

$^1/_2$ cup light miso

1 gallon water

1. Place all the ingredients in a 6-quart stockpot over high heat and bring to a boil. Decrease the heat to low and simmer for $1^1/_2$ to 2 hours, periodically skimming off any fat and impurities that rise to the surface.

2. Pour the stock mixture through a fine-mesh strainer. Discard the vegetables and herbs and use the stock as directed.

peeling and seeding tomatoes

Prepare an ice water bath. Bring a large saucepan of water to a boil. Drop in the whole tomatoes and blanch for 1 minute, then immediately transfer to the ice water bath. When cool enough to handle, peel the tomatoes, cut in half crosswise, and gently squeeze each half to remove the seeds. Use as directed.

peeling plantains

Fill your sink with warm water. Cut off both ends of each plantain and make three or four lengthwise slits through the skin. Place the plantains in the water and soak for about 10 minutes, then peel by running your fingers under skin.

roasting corn

Hold each husked ear of corn nearly vertical. With a paring knife in your other hand, cut the corn kernels off the cob. Heat a large, dry, heavy-bottomed skillet. Place the corn in the skillet (they should be no more than two layers deep), and roast over high heat for 4 to 5 minutes, tossing continuously just until the kernels begin to smoke.

roasting chiles and bell peppers

Place the chiles or peppers on a wire rack over a grill, hold suspended over a gas flame, or set on a baking sheet under a broiler. Roast until skins are blistered and blackened all over, but before flesh becomes charred. Transfer to a bowl and cover tightly with plastic wrap. Let steam for 15 to 20 minutes. When cool enough to handle, remove the skins with your fingers or the tip of a knife. Remove and discard the seeds (unless the recipe instructs otherwise) and internal ribs, and use as directed. Warning: do not touch your face or eyes after handling chiles until you have thoroughly washed your hands. If you have sensitive skin, wear rubber gloves when handling chiles.

toasting spices and seeds

Place the spices or seeds in a dry skillet over low heat. Toast, stirring frequently, for about 1 minute, or until fragrant. Alternatively, place on a baking sheet and toast in a 350° oven for 5 to 7 minutes, or until fragrant.

gLossary

This glossary is based on Spanish words and terms that refer to Latin American ingredients and foods. Keep in mind that some of the ingredient names will vary from country to country.

ACHIOTE: Also known as annatto. Brick-red seeds of a tree native to the New World, with a mildly acidic, orangelike flavor. Used as a natural coloring to give a yellowish tint to foods, including butter and cheese.

ANCHO: Dried form of the poblano chile. Has sweet, fruity tones and mild heat.

ARROZ: Spanish word for rice.

BACALAO: Dried salt cod. Popular throughout Latin America. It should be boiled in several changes of water to remove the salt. Buy the boneless type.

BONIATO: Tuber also known as white sweet potato, Florida yam, and camote. It looks like a sweet potato on the outside, but is shorter and rounder and has white, sweetish, mealy flesh. The boniato is usually large, averaging $1^1/_2$ to 2 pounds. Scrub well before using.

CACHUCHA: Tiny, round chile also known as aji dulce. Usually green, with very little heat but a pungent aroma and an acidic, slightly fruity flavor.

CALABAZA: Also called the West Indian pumpkin. A large, round, sweet squash, resembling a pumpkin (for which it can be substituted) in its size and orange flesh. Firm texture and sweet flavor.

CHAYOTE: Light green, pear-shaped squashlike vegetable with smooth skin. Has crisp and mild flavor. Also known as mirlitons.

CHICHA DE JORA: Beer made from corn, usually blue corn. Available in Latin American markets. Substitute 12 ounces of beer mixed with 3 ounces of apple cider.

CHIPOTLE: Smoked jalapeño chile. Available canned in *adobo* sauce and dried.

CHORIZO: Spicy, hard Spanish pork sausage. Substitute salami. Not to be confused with spicy Mexican chorizo, which is made with fresh pork and is sold in sausage, patty, or bulk form.

COCONUT MILK: Liquid prepared from the meat of fresh coconuts blended with water and strained (or heated and strained). It is most easily available canned.

CONCH: Mollusk (pronounced "conk") particularly popular in Florida and the Caribbean. The tough but flavorful meat must first be tenderized before cooking.

CULANTRO: Type of cilantro with long, flat leaf. Also known as *receo* or *culantrio.*

DENDÊ OIL: Red, acidic oil extracted from palm nuts.

DRIED SHRIMP: Tiny dehydrated shrimp with intense flavor. Available whole or in powdered form.

EPAZOTE: Pungent Mexican herb available fresh and dried (use fresh if possible).

FRIJOLES: Spanish word for beans.

HEARTS OF PALM: Also known as palmitos. Tender ivory-colored shoots of a type of palm. Available fresh and canned in Latin American and gourmet markets.

HUACATAY: Black mint from Peru. Substitute fresh mint mixed with a leaf or two of cilantro.

HUITLACOCHE: Fungus that grows in the kernels of corn, making them morph into irregular-shaped gray-black mounds. Has earthy flavor often likened to mushrooms or truffles.

MALANGA: Starchy root vegetable popular throughout Latin America and used much like a potato. Nutty, earthy flavor; the yellow-to-red flesh turns gray when cooked. Also known as yautia and taro.

MARISCOS: Spanish word for shellfish.

MASA HARINA: Lime-processed, dried ground corn that's available in fine and coarse grinds.

MOJO: Spicy (not hot) sauce, particularly popular in Cuba, usually served with cooked foods. Typically made with garlic, citrus juice, oil, and at least one type of herb.

PAPA: Spanish word for potato.

PINTÓN: A semiripe plantain.

PISCO: Peruvian grape liqueur similar to the Italian grappa.

PLANTAIN: Plátano in Spanish. A member of the banana family that is always used cooked. Sweet bananalike flavor with a brownish black skin when ripe; starchy in flavor with yellow skin that's freckled or spotted when semiripe; green skin in unripe state. See page 121 for instructions on peeling.

POBLANO: Fresh green chile especially popular in Mexico and Central America. In its dried form it's called the ancho chile.

POLLO: Spanish word for chicken.

POZOLE: Lime-processed, dried whole corn, cooked until it becomes tender and puffed up. Also known as hominy.

QUESO BLANCO: Salty, firm, white cheese similar to mozzarella or Muenster. Common in Latin American cooking and available in Latin American and gourmet markets.

QUESO FRESCO: Soft, crumbly, mild white cheese similar to ricotta or farmer's cheese. Does not melt well.

QUINOA (Pronounced "KEEN-wah") A tiny, ancient grainlike seed, cultivated by the Incas that's still grown extensively in the Andean region of South America. High in protein and nutrients. Used like rice or couscous.

SOFRITO: Mixture of puréed, sautéed onions, garlic, and bell peppers, used as a flavoring base for soups, stews, and other dishes.

YUCA: Starchy root vegetable popular throughout Latin America. To peel the long, tubular roots, hold in one hand and make broad slashing motions down the tuber with a heavy-duty, large knife. (A regular vegetable peeler will not work.)

sources for ingredients, books, and kitchenware

Burns Farms
16158 Hillside Circle
Montverde, FL 34756
(407) 469-4490
Huitlacoche.

Cost Plus
(510) 893-7300
Kitchenware, bowls, ladles, spices and other specialty ingredients, and cookbooks. Call for the location of a store near you.

Coyote Cafe General Store
132 West Water Street
Santa Fe, NM 87501
(800) 866-4695
Dried beans, chiles, canned chipotles, masa harina, spices.

Crate & Barrel
(888) 249-4155
Kitchenware, bowls, ladles, and cookbooks. Call for the location of a store near you.

Dallas Mozzarella Co.
2944 Elm Street
Dallas, TX 75266
(800) 798-2954
Queso fresco.

Dean & Deluca
560 Broadway
New York, NY 10012
(212) 431-1691
Spices and beans. Call for a catalog.

Gallina Canyon Ranch
P.O. Box 706
Abiquiu, NM 87510
(505) 685-4888 (also fax)
Gourmet and rare beans and chiles. Call for a list of available foods.

Kitchen Arts and Letters
1435 Lexinton Avenue
New York, NY 10128
(212) 876-5550
Cookbooks, including foreign editions.

Penzey's Spice House, Ltd.
(414) 768-8799
Spices. Call for a catalog.

Pier 1 Imports
(800) PIER101
Kitchenware, bowls, ladels, and cookbooks. Call for the location of a store near you.

Sur La Table
(800) 243-0852
Kitchenware, bowls, ladles, and cookbooks. Call for a catalog.

Williams-Sonoma
(800) 541-2233
Kitchenware, bowls, ladles, spices and other specialty ingredients, and cookbooks. Call for a catalog.

index

125

128